Next Generation Email Security: AI Based Spam Detection

Published 2026 by River Publishers
River Publishers
Broagervej 10, 9260 Gistrup, Denmark
www.riverpublishers.com

Distributed exclusively by Routledge
605 Third Avenue, New York, NY 10017, USA
4 Park Square, Milton Park, Abingdon, Oxon OX14 4RN

Next Generation Email Security: AI Based Spam Detection / by Ramjee Prasad, Vikas S Kadam, Vandana Rohokale.

Routledge is an imprint of the Taylor & Francis Group, an informa business

ISBN 978-87-4381-037-7 (paperback)

ISBN 978-87-4381-039-1 (online)

ISBN 978-87-4381-038-4 (ebook master)

ISBN 978-87-4381-041-4 (ePub)

DOI: 10.1201/9788743810384

A Publication in the River Publishers Rapids Series in *Computer Engineering and Information Science and Technology*

Next Generation Email Security: AI Based Spam Detection

Ramjee Prasad

Founder President, CTIF Global Capsule (CGC), Denmark

Vikas S Kadam

Marathwada Mitra Mandal's College of Engineering Karvenagar, Pune Maharashtra, India

Vandana Rohokale

Sinhgad Institute of Technology and Science Narhe, Pune, India

River Publishers

Routledge
Taylor & Francis Group
NEW YORK AND LONDON

Contents

Preface

Email remains one of the most widely used and trusted forms of digital communication. Yet, the same strength that makes it indispensable has also made it a primary target for cyber threats. From unsolicited messages to highly deceptive phishing attempts, email spam continues to challenge the integrity, security, and efficiency of online communication. The growing sophistication of spam techniques demands equally advanced and adaptive detection mechanisms.

This book, *Next Generation Email Security: AI Based Spam Detection*, presents a comprehensive exploration of both traditional and emerging solutions for combating email spam. Beginning with the fundamentals—including the origins, types, and early techniques for filtering spam—the book moves towards advanced frameworks powered by *artificial intelligence, machine learning, deep learning, and quantum computing.*

We introduce and evaluate two innovative approaches in detail:

- The *fitness-oriented levy improvement-based dragonfly algorithm (FLI-DA)*, which integrates deep learning with a metaheuristic optimization strategy for robust feature selection and classification.
- The *adaptive capsule network model optimized with grey-sailfish optimization (G-SFO)*, an automated framework designed to enhance accuracy and resilience in spam detection.

Alongside these, the book examines *quantum machine learning paradigms*, such as quantum support vector machines, quantum neural networks, and variational quantum algorithms, offering insights into how quantum technologies can overcome the limitations of classical spam detection methods.

The structure of the book ensures a logical progression—from understanding the problem space, reviewing existing detection models, presenting novel approaches, analyzing performance, and finally, exploring future directions. Rigorous comparative analyses, experimental validations, and discussion of open challenges provide readers with both academic depth and practical relevance.

This work is intended for a diverse audience: researchers and graduate students in computer science and cybersecurity, as well as industry professionals and policymakers seeking to understand and apply AI-based security mechanisms in practice.

We extend our sincere gratitude to colleagues, students, and collaborators who have contributed through valuable discussions and feedback. It is our hope that this book will serve not only as a reference for current practices but also as a catalyst for innovation in securing digital communication against next-generation threats.

Prof. Ramjee Prasad

Dr. Vikas Kadam

Dr. Vandana Rohokale

Aims and Objectives

Aims

- To present advanced AI-driven approaches for spam and phishing detection.
- To integrate machine learning, deep learning, and metaheuristics in secure email systems.
- To explore the potential of quantum machine learning in future cybersecurity.

Objectives

- Review classical spam detection techniques and their limitations.
- Develop and evaluate novel frameworks (FLI-DA, G-SFO–ACapsNet).
- Provide comparative performance analyses on benchmark datasets.
- Identify open research challenges and suggest future directions.

Acknowledgement

I express my sincere gratitude to Dr. Vandana Rohokale and Prof. Ramjee Prasad for their invaluable contribution, guidance, constant encouragement, and scholarly insights that shaped this book. I am equally thankful to Dr. Sangappa M. Biradar for his support and constructive suggestions throughout this work.

On a personal note, I extend heartfelt thanks to my wife, Mrs. Kalpana Kadam, and my son, Hridhaan, whose patience, love, and motivation have been my strength. I also deeply acknowledge the blessings and support of my family members, who stood by me at every stage of this journey.

Finally, I am grateful to River Publishers for recognizing and appreciating my contribution, and for providing a platform to bring this work to the research and academic community.

Dr. Vikas Kadam

About the Authors

Dr. Ramjee Prasad's accolades include authored books, chapters, 200+ peer-reviewed publications, and leadership roles in EU and US research initiatives. His career is defined by a relentless focus on secure, sustainable, and socially responsible solutions, principles he continues to advance through his entrepreneurial ventures and global partnerships. Ramjee Prasad, Fellow IEEE, IET, IETE, and WWRF, is a former Professor Emeritus of Future Technologies for Business Ecosystem Innovation (FT4BI) in the Department of Business Development and Technology, Aarhus University, Herning, Denmark. He is the Founder President of the CTIF Global Capsule (CGC) and the Founder Chairman of the Global ICT Standardization Forum for India, established in 2009. He was honored by the University of Rome "Tor Vergata," Italy as a Distinguished Professor of the Department of Clinical Sciences and Translational Medicine in 2016. He is an Honorary Professor at the University of Cape Town, South Africa and the University of KwaZulu-Natal, South Africa, and also an Adjunct Professor at Birsa Institute of Technology, Sindri, Jharkhand, India. He received Pravasi Bhartiya Samman Puraskaar (Emigrant Indian Honor Award by the Indian President) in 2023 and the Ridderkorset of Dannebrogordenen (Knight of the Dannebrog) in 2010 from the Danish Queen for the internationalization of top-class telecommunication research and education. He has received several international awards such as the IEEE Communications Society Wireless Communications Technical Committee Recognition Award in 2003 for making a contribution in the field of "Personal, Wireless and Mobile Systems and Networks," Telenor's Research Award in 2005 for impressive merits, both academic and organizational within the field of wireless and personal communication, and 2014 IEEE AESS Outstanding Organizational Leadership Award for "Organizational Leadership in developing and globalizing the CTIF (Center for TeleInFrastruktur) Research Network". He has been the Project Coordinator of several EC projects, namely, MAGNET, MAGNET Beyond, and eWALL. He has published more than 50 books, 1000 plus journal and conference publications, more than 15 patents, over 150 Ph.D. Graduates and a larger number of masters (over 250). Several of his students are today's worldwide telecommunication leaders themselves

Dr. Vikas Kadam is an accomplished researcher and Associate Professor in the Information Technology Department at Marathwada Mitra Mandal's College of Engineering, Pune. His research primarily focuses on cybersecurity, machine learning, and deep learning algorithms, with a special emphasis on spam detection using advanced machine learning techniques. He has contributed significantly to the field through several high-impact publications, including "Enhancement of Email Spam Detection Using Improved Deep Learning Algorithms for Cyber Security" published in the Journal of Computer Security (2022) and "A Hybrid Meta-Heuristic-Based Multi-Objective Feature Selection with Adaptive Capsule Network for Automated Email Spam Detection" in the International Journal of Intelligent Robotics and Applications (2022). His latest work, "Designing a Novel Framework of Email Spam Detection Using an Improved Heuristic Algorithm and Dual-Scale Feature Fusion-Based Adaptive Convolution Neural Network", was published in Information Security Journal: A Global Perspective (2025). Dr. Kadam holds a Ph.D. in Spam Detection Using Machine Learning Algorithms and was recognized for his excellence with the EMCÂš Star Performer Award in 2015. His research continues to contribute toward enhancing cybersecurity frameworks and intelligent systems, helping address critical challenges in digital communication security.

Vandana Rohokale received her B.Eng. degree in Electronics Engineering in 1997 from Pune University, Maharashtra, India. She received her master's degree in Electronics in 2007 from Shivaji University, Kolhapur, Maharashtra, India. She received her Ph.D. degree in Wireless Communication in 2013 from CTIF, Aalborg University, Denmark. She completed her post doctorate from ARHUS University under the guidance of Prof. Ramjee Prasad in 2023. She is presently working as Professor and Vice Principal in Sinhgad Institute of Technology and Science, Pune, Maharashtra, India. Her teaching experience is around 28 years. She has published four books with international publishers. She has published around 60 plus papers in various international journals and conferences. Her research interests include cooperative wireless communications, adhoc and cognitive networks, physical layer security, digital signal processing, information theoretic security and its applications, cyber security, artificial intelligence and machine learning, quantum computing, etc.

List of Abbreviations

URLs	Uniform resource locators
LSTM	Long short term neural network
CNN	Convolutional neural network
CFC	Concentration based feature construction
BPNN	Back-propagation neural network
DNN	Deep neural network
BERT	Bidirectional encoder representations from transformers
BiLSTM	Bidirectional long short term memory
k-NN	k-nearest neighbours
NB	Naïve Bayes
GloVe	Global vectors
Bi-RNN	Bi-directional recurrent neural network
Conv1D	One dimensional convolutional layer
MOGA-CNN-DLAS	Multi-objective GA and CNN-based deep learning Architectural scheme
DenseNet121	Densely connected convolutional networks
VGG16	Visual Geometry Group
ResNet50	Residual networks
ISH	Image spam hunter
SVM	Support vector machine
FC	Fully connected
AUC	Area under the curve
AUC-ROC	AUC-receiver operating characteristic curve
A-CapsNet	Adaptive capsule network
WHT	Walsh–Hadamard transform
FDA	Fisher discriminate analysis
TF-IDF	Term frequency-inverse document frequency
TV	Term variance
G-SFO	Grey-sail fish optimization

MOFS	Multi-objective feature selection
HKSVM	Hybrid kernel based support vector machine
LCS	Learning classifier systems
GELS	Gravitational emulation local search algorithm
GA	Genetic algorithm
DF	Document frequency
IG	Information gain
ELM	Extreme learning machine
SCA	Sine–cosine algorithm
RF	Random forest
DT	Decision tree
MLP	Multilayer perceptron
PSO	Particle swarm optimization
MNB-GA	Multinomial naïve Bayes with genetic algorithm
HHO	Harris Hawks optimizer
BDA	Binary dragonfly algorithm
EO	Equilibrium optimizer
SO	Seagull optimization
MPA	Marine predators algorithm
TPR	True positive rate
FPR	False positive rate
IDR	Integrated detection rate
ABC	Artificial bee colony
LR	Logistic regression
WOA	Whale optimization algorithm
WCFS	Water cycle feature selection
MOGOA	Multi-objective grasshopper optimization algorithm
EGOAs	Enhanced grasshopper optimization algorithm
NN	Neural network
NSA	Negative selection algorithm
LOF	Local outlier factor
ALO	Antlion optimization
DE	Differential evolution
AIS	Artificial immune system
KHO	Krill herd optimization
DCA	Dendritic cell algorithm
CNSA–FFO	Clustered NSA and fruit fly optimization
CCM	Cluster-based classification model
LDA	Latent Dirichlet allocation
SOAP	Social network aided personalized
SF	Symbiotic filtering

CF	Collaborative-based filtering
CBF	Content-based filtering
ENN	Edited nearest neighbors
OSN	Online Social Networks
PLSA	Probabilistic latent semantic analysis
SWN	Senti Word Net
LDAs	Latent semantic analysis
BoW	Bag of words
PCADR	Principal component analysis document reconstruction
PCs	Principle components
PCA	Principal component analysis
CFS	Correlation feature selection
PC	Personal computer
ATM	Automated teller machine
WWW	World Wide Web
GAM	Google Android market
MUA	Mail user agent
MSA	Mail submission agent
DNS	Domain name system
MTA	Mail transfer agent
SMTP	Simple mail transfer protocol
MDA	Mail delivery agent
GLCM	Gray-level co-occurrence matrix
FLI-DA	Fitness oriented levy improvement-based dragonfly Algorithm
RNN	Recurrent neural network
TV	Term variance
ANNs	Artificial neural networks
FPGA	Field programmable gate array
GPU	Graphics processing unit
CRNN	Convolutional recurrent neural network
GWO	Grey wolf optimizer
E-mail	Electronic mail
WHTM	Walsh–Hadamard transform matrix
NPV	Negative predictive value
FDR	False discovery rate
MCC	Mathews correlation coefficient
FNR	False negative rate
FPR	False positive rate

CHAPTER

1

Introduction

1.1 Emergence of Online Social Networks

Email spam has recently become a growing concern among internet users. The increasing rate of spam has heightened worries within online communities. Various approaches, both technical and non-technical, have been developed to address the challenges in email spam detection. This chapter delves into the issues of email categorization in spam filtering models, given that spam significantly impacts web users. This research suggests several solutions for filtering spam emails, highlighting their advancements and limitations. Additionally, it explores various spam filtering methods. Spam, defined as unsolicited messages sent to users' inboxes, creates numerous problems, including security risks and legal concerns, and consumes critical resources like bandwidth, storage, and productivity. Consequently, there is a growing demand for automated spam filtering techniques. Professionals are therefore working to implement highly effective spam detection frameworks to reduce spam. Spammers use spam campaigns, malware, and botnets to send unwanted messages freely. To address this, this book proposes a novel, automated email spam detection framework utilizing deep structured architectures to tackle challenges in traditional spam detection techniques.

Today, social media has evolved into a powerful platform for sharing real-life connections, interests, activities, and personal backgrounds through visual technology. Social networks maintain basic user information, including profile photos, social connections, and additional details about their education

DOI: 10.1201/9788743810384-1

and career. Over time, online social networks (OSNs) have gained popularity, becoming a more integrated part of everyday life. Initially, email served as the primary online network for sharing information across different email addresses. However, with the advent of smartphones, people now have a wide range of social media options such as Twitter, Instagram, Snapchat, Facebook, and Tumblr. Figure 1.1 illustrates popular OSN interfaces like Facebook and Twitter.

Many people, including celebrities, use multiple OSN platforms to share their daily activities, personal thoughts, and plans. The abundance of information shared on OSNs has become essential for global companies and organizations to distribute their content.

With recent advances in various OSN functionalities, users are now more inclined to share updates, such as videos and photos, due to their large followings. Additionally, some OSNs introduce new features to allow content to be shared across platforms. For example, users can link Facebook and Twitter to post updates automatically, and some websites include buttons that let followers share pages across different OSNs.

1.2 Challenges of Social Network Security

Professionals have developed various technologies and policies to combat spam activities across the web. Email systems, in particular, are highly targeted by spammers, leading to the creation of advanced techniques to detect spam in both email and social networks. The popularity of OSNs has also made them fertile ground for spammers who aim to advertise or post malicious content on user profiles. Data shared on social networks lacks guaranteed security, exposing users to increased vulnerability. Despite secured settings, webpages often share user information, giving spammers access. Personal data on OSNs can be exploited for attacks, often through posts that friends share, malware downloads, or links to unsafe sites. Social media sites are frequently targeted by malicious actors, such as competitors and hackers, who exploit user data for targeted attacks. To address rising spam levels, experts have developed several approaches for effective spam detection and categorization.

In content-based spam detection, experts use the TF-IDF framework, focusing on word characteristics and frequency differences across documents. For link categorization, users may rely on page rank systems, which validate links through hyperlinks. Spammers, however, adapt to these methods by using link-based ranking techniques to boost target page scores. Through the TF-IDF

Figure 1.1: Samples of Facebook and Twitter interference.

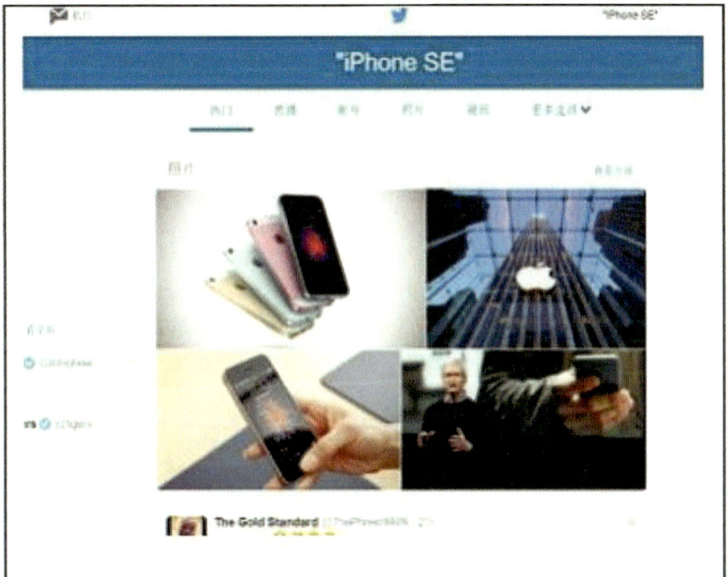

Facebook interference

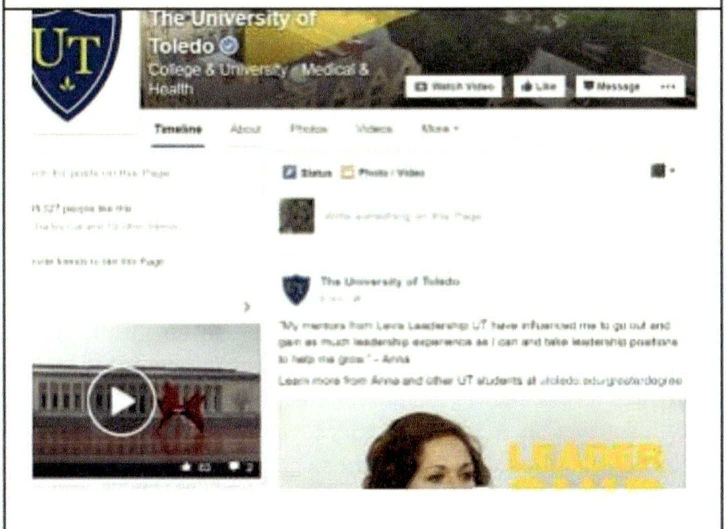

Twitter interference

model, spam words are identified within content, and spam pages often rank similarly across various searches.

Information from social networks can be exploited to craft attacks outside OSNs. Statistics show that around 10% of tweets on Twitter are spam, and Facebook blocks about 200 million malicious attempts daily. A 2008 survey revealed that 83% of social media users had encountered unknown messages and friend requests, indicating widespread spam in social networks. Although companies have developed more anti-spam techniques, spam volume continues to rise, often outpacing user growth. Some hackers even alter social media platform code to embed malicious content, which may include data on third-party apps and advertisements. Shortened URLs on sites like Twitter and Facebook can lead to malicious sites, endangering personal data, especially given how easily tweets reach wide audiences, making Twitter particularly vulnerable.

Spam policies on social networks pose ongoing challenges and, without adequate policies, users struggle to protect their privacy. OSNs still face obstacles in safeguarding user data. Recently, Google removed about a hundred malicious apps from its GAM that had been stealing and selling users' private information. Social media platforms have introduced additional features to improve security, with options on Twitter and Facebook to report spam content, prompting quick removal if deemed spam. Spam filter systems on various social platforms have improved significantly, helping detect and address spam across OSNs.

1.3 Email spam: An Issue in Cyber Security

Advancements in email spam analysis models and increased internet usage have led to the categorization of spam mail, making these models popular for their reliability, easy access, and speed. With just one click, users can connect with anyone globally at any time. Due to factors like low cost, many people now use email for commercial purposes, resulting in an influx of unwanted emails in users' inboxes, known as spam. These spam emails come from various sources, such as companies or individuals with different motives, and are often highly intrusive. Spam mail presents several issues, starting with wasted resources, as downloading spam consumes company bandwidth and network capacity. For many companies, internet and network costs are significant, so reducing such waste is critical. Additionally, spam creates difficulties for users by complicating efforts to install antivirus solutions. Ultimately, spam emails are a nuisance, consuming time, reducing productivity, and impacting system efficiency.

1.4 Sources of Email Spam

In recent days, spammers have employed different techniques to attain the mail address of the user. Different techniques used by the spammers are detailed as follows.

Email addresses on site: Most of the spammers utilized specific software to identify the spider website for collecting the email address. To resolve these types of email collection other email links are utilized to get connected with the webmaster.

Auto reply message: The auto reply options in email messages are highly attractive among spammers. Moreover, it is a kind of spamming technique to send more messages to a large number of email addresses. If the spammer gets any response mail from the user they mark the email address as existing. Next, the spammer utilizes the email address for sending spam emails to the user not using the auto reply option in the mail.

Common email addresses: Some examples of common email addresses are webmaster @, admin @, into @, and so on. These types of common addresses are utilized to send spam emails randomly. This is the best technique for the spammers to obtain essential data like company details, admin contact, and so on.

Subscription: Spammers generally smell for the latest mail addresses using highly advanced software systems. If the web customer subscribes to a new website the spammer immediately uses the basic email address of the user.

Guest book: In this case, the users leave a message or comment on the website from their basic email address. This procedure is not recommended for the guest book due to the presence of the spammer who frequently checks for new primary email addresses.

1.5 Types of Spam

The term "spam" is commonly used to describe unwanted emails, and it's important to recognize different types of spam.

Commercial spam mail: The most common type of spam, aimed at promoting a company's products, services, or goods. These emails often include topics such as personal finance, politics, health, entertainment, IT training, education, and even anti-spam solutions.

Chain letters: One of the earliest types of spam, chain letters encourage users to forward the email to multiple people, often under the pretense of gaining good luck. Unlike commercial spam, these emails are simply labeled as unwanted.

Scams: Many scams are conducted through email, including popular schemes like the "African nation" or "Nigerian prince" scams. These messages often claim to involve money laundering, suspicious business proposals, or fraudulent legal offers from supposedly ordinary individuals.

Malware proliferation: This type of spam is designed to spread malware, often disguised as messages related to software licenses, tax information, delivery notifications, or bank transactions. These emails typically contain infected links that can compromise attachments and websites, leading to malware infections.

Phishing attacks: Phishing emails attempt to obtain sensitive information from users by mimicking legitimate company emails. They ask for details like usernames, passwords, account numbers, phone numbers, and ATM PINs through links that appear to be from trustworthy sites. Phishing emails often come from banking-related services like PayPal, eBay, or other financial applications, as shown in Figure 1.2

1.6 Spam Avoiding Techniques

Numerous research efforts have proposed various solutions to address spam-related issues. While some techniques offer innovative ideas, they have a lower success rate compared to traditional methods due to design complexities. Solutions for handling spam emails can be divided into two main types:

- Non-technical solutions.
- Technical solutions.

1.6.1 Non-technical techniques

Various issues in spam prevention solutions stem from recipients' responses, some of which are outlined below. This approach does not involve specific tools but relies on users and organizations taking action against spam senders.

Figure 1.2: Pictorial representation of a phishing attack.

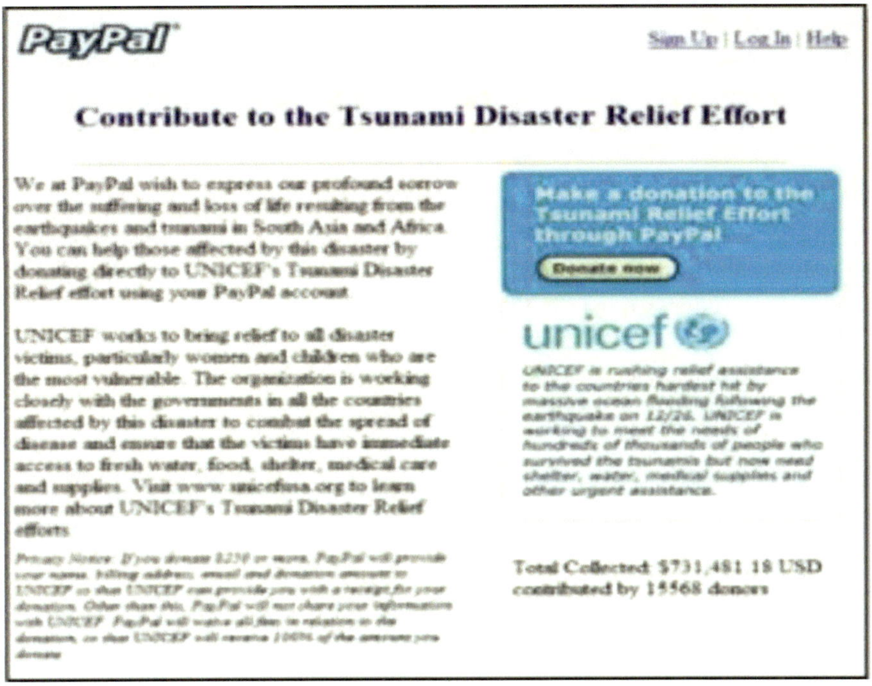

Effective awareness among email users can significantly improve the success of these solutions.

When a web user approves incoming email, it is first sent to the mail user agent (MUA) and then forwarded to the mail submission agent (MSA). The MSA checks the domain name system (DNS) for mail exchange (MX) records from the sender's host. Once identified, the MSA communicates with the mail transfer agent (MTA) to send the email via the simple mail transfer protocol (SMTP). The MTA then forwards the email to the mail delivery agent (MDA) to deliver it to the recipient's mailbox.

Key non-technical solutions include:

Recipient revolt: This response involves other users reacting angrily to spam senders. It helps legitimate companies avoid spam practices.

Customer revolt: Since many spam emails are advertisements, customers may respond by following the company's suggested revolt policies, such as adhering to appropriate publishing policies and data collection standards. Challenges in this approach include:

- Differentiating between valid and invalid complaints.
- High rates of incorrect complaints.

Vigilante attack: This method involves sending denial-of-service (DoS) attacks or mail bombs to spam addresses, potentially deterring spammers from targeting the same addresses again. Limitations include:

- Ethical concerns and potential complexities.
- The difficulty of accurately identifying spammers.

Hiding email addresses: Using two separate email addresses, where the primary address receives all emails and forwards them to a secondary, private address accessible only to trusted users. Drawbacks include:

- Limited usability with multiple email addresses.
- Lack of direct spam prevention.

A typical non-technical approach for common mailing procedures is illustrated in Figure 1.3.

Hide your email address: A useful approach to protect privacy is to use two separate email addresses. The primary address receives all incoming emails, allowing the user to filter them before forwarding to a secondary address, which is only accessible to verified contacts. However, this method has some drawbacks:

- It can be challenging to manage with a limited number of email addresses.
- It does not directly prevent spam from reaching the inbox.

1.6.2 Technical techniques

In spam detection processes, technical solutions typically involve isolating one spam email in a user's account, with spam identification models applied to filter it out. These spam identification methods discourage spammers and add complexity to their activities. Additionally, online communities are generally

Figure 1.3: Non-technical procedure for common mailing.

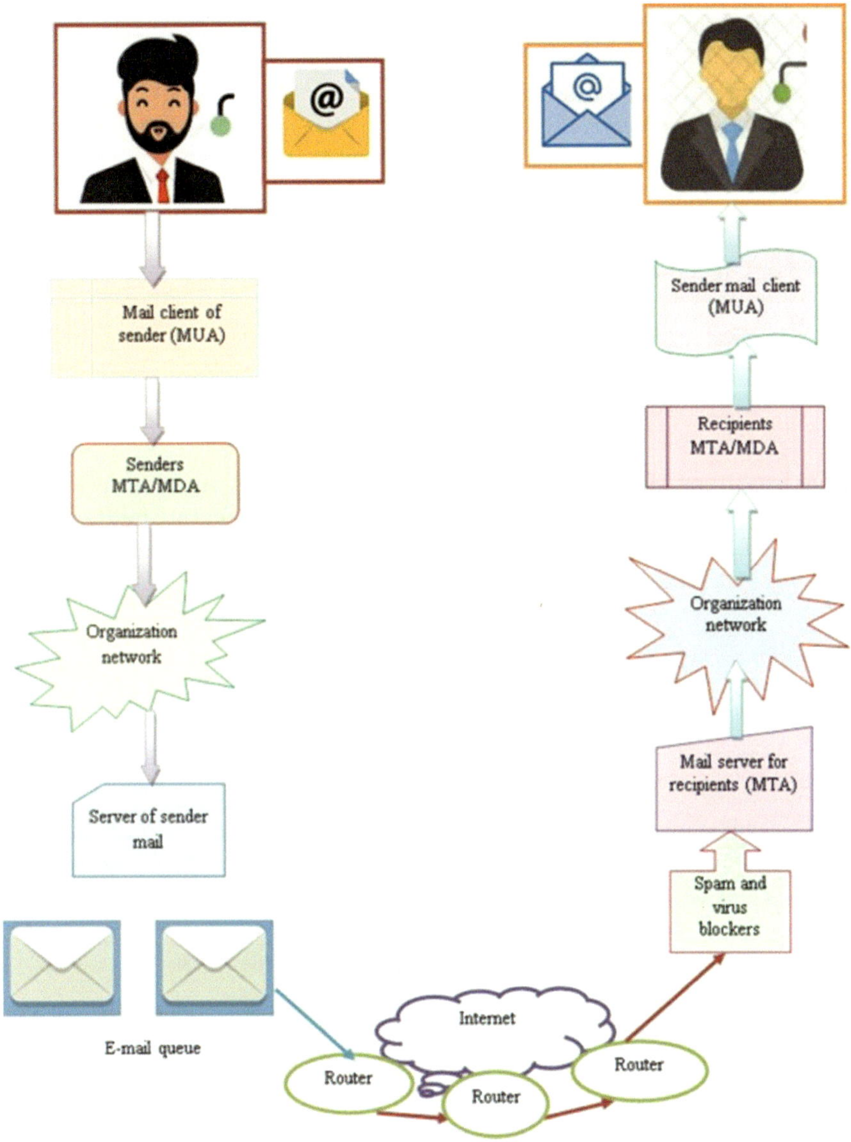

aware of spam issues and professionals anticipate highly effective models, though active research efforts to address these challenges have been limited. The following technical solutions address these issues:

Domain filters: Specialized programs are integrated with systems to handle spam from specific domains, effectively differentiating spam from legitimate emails. However, challenges include:

- Reducing email communication limits.
- Spammers sometimes use legitimate domains.

Blacklisting: This method excludes unknown email addresses, relying on databases to track known spammers by filtering their emails. While effective in some cases, it can mistakenly filter out genuine users. Key limitations include:

- Increased overhead for users as databases need constant monitoring.
- Complications in updating distributed databases and recognizing changes in email addresses, as these are often not reflected in outdated databases.

White list filters: This approach learns users' contact lists, allowing only known contacts' emails through while routing other emails to a separate folder. Advantages include a spam- free inbox with only familiar contacts' emails. However, challenges include:

- User configuration programs need to analyze contacts.
- If a user's email address changes, it may not be recognized by the system.
- Delays can occur for emails from new contacts due to limited visibility within the system, impacting user interactions.

Rules-based: Professionals analyze spam emails to establish patterns in words and phrases, creating rules for effective spam detection. Weights are assigned to these rules based on their classification accuracy. Limitations involve:

- The need for human oversight, as rules may become outdated due to spam tactics constantly evolving.
- Continuous human intervention is required to update the system and improve spam filtering based on new patterns in contextual email classes.
- Overall, these solutions are complex and require ongoing adjustments and supervision for optimal spam control.

1.7 Filtering Techniques for Email Spam Removal

The automatic spam filtering method is known as a simple document feature categorization model. This document categorization approach involves two

Figure 1.4: Structural presentation of a document problem classification framework.

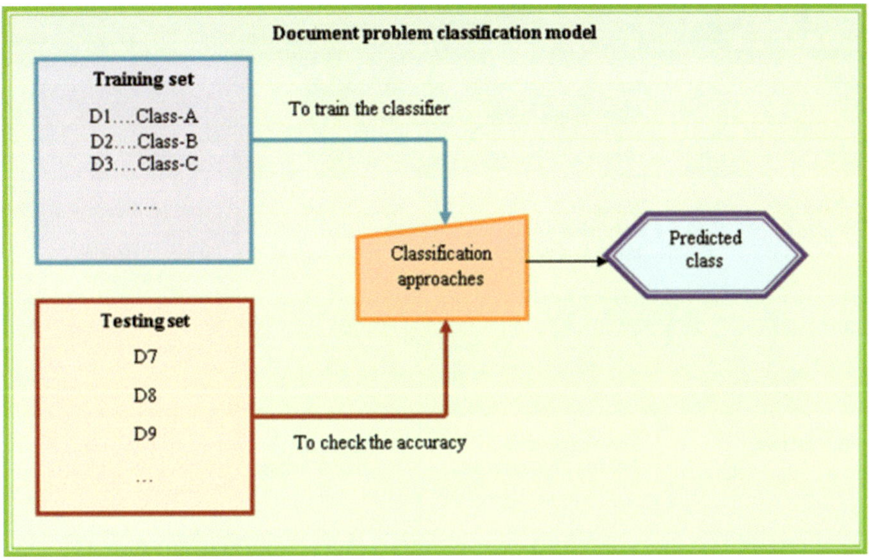

types of documents. The first type, the training set, contains documents with predefined class labels, which are used by the classifier to analyze data patterns. The second type is a set of unlabeled documents used for testing purposes. This set includes samples from real-world scenarios, which are processed in the classification phase for accurate categorization. In spam identification, the model must classify documents into multiple categories, such as spam and legitimate. The filtering process takes an email document as input, analyzes its patterns, and uses these to classify it into the appropriate category. After the learning phase, the model can effectively identify and filter out spam emails with high accuracy. Issues related to document classification are shown in Figure 1.4.

The primary role of a document categorization framework is to gather data from various applications. It is crucial to execute document extraction in an efficient and timely manner. In this framework, each web page is treated as a document, containing elements like images, text, etc., and is commonly used to organize documents in digital libraries. The document filtering process involves tasks such as indexing, searching, web filtering, and classifying web pages. Table 1.1 lists the various spam filtering techniques used in this process.

Table 1.1: Various spam filtering models with advantages and disadvantages.

Spam filter type	Technique	Advantages	Limitations
Copyright token	Email users apply a copyright token as an anti-spam measure.	Only emails with valid tokens are received.	Spammers can replicate the token in their emails, reducing effectiveness.
Challenge/ response	Blocks unauthorized emails until a response is received.	Allows trusted senders to bypass once they respond.	Can inconvenience new genuine senders by requiring a response for each message.
Password filter	Requires a password within the email, which then allows it to pass through the filter.	Only emails containing the password are permitted.	Legitimate emails lacking the password are blocked.
Blacklist filter	Blocks emails from designated barred senders.	Effectively stops known spam emails.	Ineffective at blocking new spam from previously unknown senders.
Community-based	Filters emails based on community consensus.	Screens emails before they reach the user.	Resource-intensive, requiring substantial bandwidth and code, which can overload server resources during transmission and increase processing demand.

1.8 Existing Email Spam Detection Models

Currently, spam is widespread across various platforms like forum posts, blog comments, social networks, emails, instant messaging bots, video comments, and pop-up ads. The complexity of spam has increased with advancements in communication technology. To address this, researchers have developed effective spam filtering methods, especially for spam emails in the SMTP time series (Table 1.2). Many spam filtering techniques use machine learning, achieving high performance rates with established classifiers in spam detection. Later, rule-based models leveraging rough set theory were introduced to handle distinct categories, such as spam and legitimate classes. In spam filtering, the naïve Bayes (NB) classifier is widely used due to its simplicity and its effectiveness in detecting spam.

Table 1.2: Different types of email spam detection models

Technique	Advantages	Limitations
HKSVM	– Kernel functions in the detection model adapt well to various tasks. – Accurately organizes high-dimensional regions.	– Requires a large dataset for effective results and needs further improvements in efficacy.
NN (neural networks)	– Enhances detection accuracy, recall, and precision rates for spam.	– Does not achieve a high categorization rate in terms of efficacy.
SVM	– Provides a reliable, flexible, and efficient solution with better performance than traditional models.	– Produces less effective results when analyzing data with significant noise.
Ensemble technique	– Increases system efficacy and achieves a high accuracy rate.	– Ineffective in analyzing both email bodies and subject lines due to differing clustering processes.
ANN (artificial neural network)	– Simple to implement with a parallel architecture and adaptable computational framework.	– Requires substantial training data for real-world applications.
GA (genetic algorithm)	– Uses a character recognition framework and effectively detects key spam features, adjusting configurations in core classifiers.	– Slows system performance due to unguided mutations and lacks validation for imbalanced datasets.
Statistical approach	– Focuses on email headers to efficiently reduce false positives.	– Not effective for certain data assumptions and can be time-consuming in problem summarization.
AIS (artificial immune system)	– Easy to understand, generalizes input data well, offers user privacy, and resists message and language variation.	– Reduces recall rate, lowers system efficiency, and requires parallel hybridization for effective spam detection.
DT (Decision Tree)	– A commonly used data mining method that identifies errors with minimal validation time.	– Difficult to interpret large trees and not typically applied in real-world scenarios.

Various versions of NB exist, including flexible Bayes, multinomial NB with Boolean attributes, multinomial NB, multivariate Bernoulli NB, and SpamAssassin's implementation, each adapted for different representation and classification needs. NB methods are fundamental in spam filtering and serve as a base in many classification models with varying success.

Support vector machine (SVM) techniques are also applied to classify message features, mapping data points into higher-dimensional spaces for classification. SVM identifies the optimal hyperplane separating classes, maximizing the distance between positive and negative classes, demonstrating effectiveness in spam filtering. Additionally, artificial neural network (ANN) models are used, consisting of interconnected artificial neurons and weighted links, primarily for training where connection weights are updated. However, ANN-based spam filters tend to underperform compared to Bayesian methods.

Another approach, the artificial immune system (AIS) technique, inspired by biological immune responses, is applied to pattern recognition and spam detection. Although AIS can handle complex cases, it often produces higher false positives. K-nearest neighbor (KNN) methods are also utilized for spam detection due to their simplicity, using voting from training samples but tend to be less effective than traditional spam identification techniques.

Finally, combining boosting techniques with weak learners has shown promising results for spam detection. Among these, Adaboost has demonstrated superior spam detection rates compared to other methods.

1.9 Summary

Email has become an inexpensive, popular, and convenient tool for effective communication within organizations and among individuals, largely replacing traditional postal services. It facilitates faster, easier communication. However, the number of unsolicited spam emails has been rising quickly, posing various issues. Recent studies indicate that 70% of emails received by users are spam. This influx of spam has hindered client opportunities and led to increased efforts to monitor and remove unwanted messages, causing further complications. In limited mailbox storage, spam clutters and wastes data transmission space, making it potentially more damaging than computer viruses. This high volume of spam has driven the development of efficient and accurate spam detection models to enhance identification rates. Security is crucial for internetusers, and spam filtering has become a priority for organizations, companies, individuals, and governments alike. Currently, inboxes are flooded with spam in various forms—such as images, colorful text, links, and videos—which can be highly disruptive. As a result, researchers have focused on creating advanced spam detection methods to accurately identify and remove spam emails. A variety of anti-spam software and filtering techniques are available online to address the challenges in email spam detection. Among these techniques, swarm intelligence is frequently used to achieve high detection accuracy in spam filtering systems.

CHAPTER

2

Email Spam Detection Models Overview

2.1 Introduction

In today's world, information sharing has become incredibly fast and accessible due to advances in communication technology. Email stands out as one of the most affordable, simple, and rapid methods of sharing information. However, emails are also vulnerable to various threats, with spam being one of the most significant. Spam refers to unwanted or irrelevant messages sent to recipients without their consent, often wasting their time and resources. Spam also poses security risks, potentially compromising host systems. Because spam can be generated from anywhere via the Internet, it can overload servers by consuming capacity and memory. Many spam emails carry viruses, Trojans, or malicious links designed to direct users to harmful websites or engage in financial fraud. Accurate spam detection in emails is therefore essential, requiring intelligent detection mechanisms to classify spam as malicious, blacklisted, or whitelisted. Spammers also use popular networking platforms to target specific audiences, placing hidden links on fan and review pages that lead users to fraudulent sites.

Classifying and managing spam is challenging, as new spam techniques continuously emerge. Spam filters are used to detect unwanted emails, though they sometimes also filter out legitimate messages. Traditional spam detection methods include heuristic and Bayesian filters, while modern techniques increasingly leverage artificial intelligence (AI) to distinguish between spam and non-spam emails by analyzing features in the email subject, header, and body. Current spam detection methods based on machine learning learn from specific features to improve classification accuracy. However, these methods face complexities due to factors like language diversity, concept drift,

DOI: 10.1201/9788743810384-2

text latency, and the subjective nature of spam, which increase processing demands.

Spam detection approaches are broadly divided into non-machine learning and machine learning categories. Non-machine learning techniques, such as blacklisting, heuristics, and signatures, provide complementary solutions by classifying incoming messages independently. Machine learning based classifiers are now commonly used to analyze email features for spam classification, though they often face issues like overfitting. Advanced spam detection methods now include deep learning techniques, such as ensemble learning, neural networks, and transfer learning, which enhance both detection accuracy and classification performance.

Email spam filtering techniques have been developed in various forms, with numerous spam detection models researched and organized into different categories as follows.

- Supervised deep learning based models
- Supervised machine learning based models
- Enhanced heuristic based models
- Unsupervised clustering based models
- Hybrid spam detection models
- Unaddressed challenges.

2.2 Supervised Deep Learning Based Models

In 2019, Jain et al. [50] developed a spam email detection technique using LSTM and CNN, incorporating knowledge bases like ConceptNet and WordNet for linguistic representation, which improved the model's performance. The accuracy and F1-score were assessed with two datasets.

In 2010, Ruan and Tan [51] presented a spam detection method using CFC and a three-layer BPNN. They used "self" and "non-self" data from gene libraries within the CFC approach for email analysis. The model, tested on Ling and PU1 corpora datasets, showed high classification accuracy and required minimal processing time.

In 2021, Sumathi and Kumar [54] combined DNN and RF to build a spam detection system. They used the RF algorithm to rank features and trained the DNN classifier using backpropagation. The approach achieved high classification accuracy by dynamically iterating the detector.

In 2022, Shaaban et al. [55] proposed a dynamic deep ensemble approach for spam detection, employing the RF classifier and convolutional layers for feature extraction, along with bagging and boosting. The model performed well on accuracy, F1-score, recall, and precision metrics compared to other algorithms.

In 2020, Gibson et al. [66] analyzed word embedding for spam classification using BERT, which utilized attention layers for context. Compared against DNN and other classifiers like k-NN and NB, BERT showed higher accuracy, validated with two datasets.

In 2022, Magdy et al. [76] introduced a deep-learning approach using three datasets with context- based features, showing classification accuracy in distinguishing three classes of spam, with low processing time for training and detection.

In 2023, Rao et al. [80] created a hybrid model that balanced datasets using SmoteTomek and NearMiss and employed word embeddings (FastText and GloVe) in a DNN structure with Bi-RNN and Conv1D. The model outperformed traditional machine learning methods in accuracy, especially for detecting social spam.

In 2022, Darling and Jacob [81] developed MOGA-CNN-DLAS for spam detection on Twitter, assessing it on metrics like recall, accuracy, and F1-score across three datasets, including a 100k dataset and ASU.

In 2023, Salama et al. [82] proposed a hybrid spam image detection model utilizing DenseNet121, InceptionV3, MobileNetV2, VGG16, and ResNet50 with SVM classifiers. Data augmentation and transfer learning increased accuracy, with ResNet50 achieving notable precision and F1-scores.

In 2022, Andresini et al. [84] suggested EUPHORIA, a multi-view deep learning method for distinguishing spam and genuine reviews, improving accuracy on datasets such as Yelp and a Hotel and Restaurant dataset.

In 2023, Muralidharan and Nissim [88] introduced a fully automated deep-learning spam email detection model analyzing headers, attachments, and bodies, which outperformed traditional models.

In 2022, Vikas and Rohokale [95] proposed a spam detection model for both text and images, using A-CapsNet with multi-objective feature selection. Image features were extracted using WHT and FDA, while text features used TF-IDF. The G-SFO algorithm optimized CapsNet parameters, achieving high spam detection accuracy as shown in experimental analysis.

2.3 Supervised Machine Learning Based Models

In 2019, Kumaresan et al. [45] developed a spam detection system using HKSVM and the S- Cuckoo search algorithm. This model extracted both image and text features from emails, employing wavelet moments and correlograms for image features, while TF-term frequency was used for text features. The S-Cuckoo algorithm optimized feature selection, and HKSVM combined hybrid kernels for classification, yielding superior results to other methods. The Spam Archive corpus, evaluated with lemm-ling and bare-ling spam, validated the classification performance.

In 2020, Gaurav et al. [48] introduced a machine-learning model for spam email detection, addressing challenges from informal text, limited data, and few datasets in traditional methods. This approach, using random forest, decision tree, and naïve Bayes, demonstrated better accuracy across three datasets compared to previous methods.

In 2018, Hassan et al. [49] explored LCS, a machine-learning approach, to identify spam in emails and SMS and analyze sentiment in movie reviews and Twitter messages. Sentiment lexicons and term frequency generated feature vectors managed by an added encoder, resulting in high spam detection performance.

In 2023, Pirozmand et al. [53] proposed a spam-filtering technique in social networks with SVM, utilizing GELS and GA for feature selection. This model showed better accuracy than other approaches.

In 2006, Wang et al. [52] designed a spam-filtering method employing odds ratio, DF, and IG for feature selection. This approach improved the online classifiers Winnow and Perceptron over naïve Bayes, yielding better detection results with lower training time.

In 2016, Zheng et al. [59] presented a supervised spam detection model using ELM, classifying users on social media as spammers or non-spammers based on behavior and text features, showing high true positive rates.

In 2020, Talaei et al. [43] minimized error in spam email detection by using SCA for feature retrieval and optimizing feature vectors for ANN training in MATLAB, achieving higher sensitivity, accuracy, and precision compared to other approaches like RF, DT, and Bayesian networks.

In 2021, Ghaleb et al. [66] developed a machine learning spam detection model using optimization algorithms to fine-tune model parameters, analyzing multiple datasets with MLP, DT, RF, SVM, and NB. GA and PSO enhanced classifier performance, with MNB-GA outperforming others.

In 2022, Mashaleh et al. [74] combined the HHO algorithm with k-NN for spam detection, resolving issues with high-dimensional data and achieving high accuracy over other methods like BDA and EO.

In 2022, Mageshkumar et al. [77] created an enhanced NB-based spam filter that uses machine learning, keywords, and semantics to improve accuracy and detect spam associated with Bayesian poisoning.

In 2019, Diale et al. [78] emphasized preprocessing to improve classification speed and accuracy, using feature reduction and extraction to prepare data for classifiers like DT C4.5, SVM, and RF, achieving strong generalization across varied data sources.

In 2021, Daisy and Begum [86] created a hybrid classifier combining Markov Random Fields with NB for spam detection. This fusion enhanced probabilistic classification, minimized processing time, and improved accuracy over other methods.

In 2019, Olusanya [96] developed an SVM-based spam detection model with optimized feature selection, achieving 94.87% accuracy in testing and outperforming previous models.

In 2018, Cohen et al. [90] proposed a model to detect spam by extracting descriptive features from email content without external tools, achieving high detection efficiency with RF classifiers and improving TPR and FPR with an IDR metric.

In 2020, Kagan and Akay [85] introduced a spam detection model using the LR Classifier and ABC, demonstrating robust performance across high-dimensional data, with superior accuracy on datasets like TurkishEmail and Enron compared to baseline methods like NB and SVM.

2.4 Enhanced Heuristic Based Models

In 2019, Shuaib et al. [42] applied the rotation forest algorithm and the Whale Optimization Algorithm (WOA) for spam email classification, analyzing the algorithm's performance both with and without feature extraction. Their model demonstrated lower false positive rates and higher accuracy compared to other methods.

In 2023, Naravajhula and Naravajula [58] explored genetic optimization and a passive-aggressive spectrum for classifying spam messages. They used an online learning algorithm for spam detection and reviewed other algorithms in spam filtering, demonstrating improved stability and effectiveness with datasets like Twitter spam, spam reviews, and SMS spam.

In 2019, Rawashdeh et al. [62] developed a model that combined Water Cycle and Simulated Annealing algorithms for feature selection in spam detection. Testing across seven datasets, their hybrid fusion algorithm reduced feature counts and improved accuracy over traditional classifiers.

In 2021, Karim et al. [64] designed a spam detection model that enhanced classification accuracy by reducing false positives and using a multi-objective genetic optimization algorithm (MOGOA) to select features. Testing on standard datasets confirmed improved accuracy and system performance.

In 2022, Ghaleb et al. [65] integrated six enhanced genetic optimization algorithms (EGOAs) with a multi-layer perceptron (MLP) for advanced email spam detection, achieving strong results on detection rate, false alarm rate, and accuracy.

In 2021, AbdulNabi et al. [68] introduced a model based on a negative selection algorithm (NSA) and particle swarm optimization (PSO) for spam detection in a client-server setup. The model's NSA-PSO combination with the local outlier factor (LOF) significantly improved classification accuracy and spam coverage.

In 2015, Idris et al. [69] introduced ALO-Boosting, an antlion optimization framework that selected optimal feature subsets for spam classification, achieving better performance than existing models when compared to algorithms like SVM, KNN, and Bagging.

In 2014, Idris and Selamat [70] improved NSA's random identifier generation using a stochastic distribution model with PSO support, enhancing spam and non-spam detector variation. Experimental results indicated a higher detection rate than standard NSA.

In 2014, Idris et al. [73] presented NSA–DE, an immune system-based spam detection model using differential evolution for detector generation. This method, which incorporated distance computations to handle overlapping detectors, outperformed standard NSA in detection accuracy.

In 2022, Sokhangoee and Rezapour [83] proposed a supervised spam detection model for online networks. They used a hybrid method of genetic algorithms and rule mining for feature selection and applied well-known classifiers to improve accuracy, achieving up to 95.24%.

In 2021, Sharaff et al. [87] proposed a Danger Theory-inspired artificial immune system (AIS) model for SMS spam filtering, using bio-inspired KHO and DCA algorithms for feature selection and optimization. The model achieved a high accuracy of 96%, along with improvements in precision, recall, and F1-score.

2.5 Unsupervised Clustering Based Models

In 2010, Katakis et al. [57] developed a framework utilizing stream clustering to update and classify data streams. This involved creating a conceptual representation where examples were mapped through a transformation function. A clustering algorithm was used to detect recurring contexts, and an incremental classifier was employed to build an ensemble for each concept in the data stream. The proposed model's effectiveness was validated on standard datasets, demonstrating that concept-specific classifiers were reliable for spam email filtering.

In 2021, Karim et al. [63] explored unsupervised learning for classifying spam and non-spam emails. The research emphasized implementing an unsupervised model using clustering strategies, integrating various algorithms based on both email content and subject headers. Clustering was performed on a binary dataset containing 22,000 entries for spam and non-spam emails, with ten unique features designed to highlight the impact of analytical email characteristics from multiple perspectives. Comparing this approach with five different clustering techniques revealed that the proposed model provided optimal clustering with higher average efficiency.

In 2019, Chikh and Chikhi [97] introduced a novel hybrid CNSA–FFO model, which utilized an NSA-based approach for spam email detection. By combining K-means Clustering within the NSA and FFO algorithm, this model enhanced the traditional NSA's performance. Experimental results on a benchmark spam dataset showed that the CNSA-FFO model achieved higher detection accuracy, reduced computational complexity, and better predictive results than NSA-PSO and standard NSA models.

In 2014, Nizamani et al. [89] proposed an advanced method for selecting optimal features for fake email detection. To assess detection accuracy, the performance of each feature was compared with other features, gradually adding more in each step. Given that fake email detection is a classification task, the method was evaluated using multiple algorithms, including CCM and advanced conventional methods. Simulations with various features and classifiers concluded that feature selection was a more significant factor than classifier choice for developing an effective fake email detection model.

2.6 Hybrid Spam Detection Models

In 2022, Rajendran et al. [41] introduced a hybrid model for detecting spam emails by leveraging email layout. This method identifies spam email formations and, based on user input, creates a spam database within the developed framework. A matching mechanism was used to classify incoming emails as spam or ham, while weights were assigned to email layout and fingerprints to reduce false positives and negatives. The model's performance was validated on a standard dataset, showing improved classification effectiveness.

In 2023, Rustam et al. [46] developed a model for spam email classification using email text features. By incorporating more features, the model achieved high accuracy, evaluated using various deep learning and machine learning methods. The study also examined data resampling effects and reported metrics such as accuracy, precision, recall, and F1-score. Logistic regression and Random Forest (RF) outperformed other algorithms.

In 2017, Shao et al. [47] created a hybrid spam detection model using dictionary learning to construct ham and spam sub-dictionaries. The model extracted local and global image features through sparse representation-based classification, assessing the maliciousness of email content. This approach categorized real versus meta-spam effectively, as demonstrated in outcome reports.

In 2012, Carlos et al. [56] developed a spam detection model focusing on ham and phishing emails, applying dimensionality reduction techniques for feature extraction. Various feature retrieval methods were tested, validated on datasets like TREC, PU1, SpamAssassin, and Ling- Spam, to gauge classification efficiency. A short profile rule was applied to filter spam emails, resulting in fast, dynamic feature extraction and effective spam classification.

In 2019, Jose and Sasidhar [60] proposed an LDA-based approach for spam detection, which captures both local and global topic distribution patterns. Performance testing on two datasets showed an enhanced F1-score compared to other methods.

In 2014, Shen and Li [61] introduced SOAP, a spam filter leveraging social network-based nodes. Each node connected to social friends to form a distributed overlay network, improving spam filtering through features like friend notification, adaptive trust, and social accuracy. SOAP showed enhanced detection efficiency based on trace data tests and proved useful in practical applications.

In 2023, Jáñez et al. [71] developed a topic-aided spam classification model, SPEMC-15K-E and SPEMC-15K-S, for 15,000 English and Spanish emails across 11 categories using agglomerative hierarchical clustering. Evaluated using BERT, Word2Vec, Bag of Words, and TF-IDF combined with SVM, NB, RF, and LR, the model demonstrated superior classification speed and performance for both languages.

In 2011, Lopes et al. [72] introduced SF, a spam filtering method using combined local filters for improved spam identification. Incorporating CF and CBF features allowed social network customization for spam filtering. Comparative testing showed SF's high resilience against focused attacks and dictionary contamination while maintaining privacy and low communication costs.

In 2023, Kumar et al. [75] developed a hybrid spam detection model for Twitter, utilizing SMOTE-ENN to balance data and improve classifier accuracy. This model optimized spam detection for OSN by analyzing different algorithms and evaluation metrics.

In 2022, Srinivasarao and Sharaff [94] proposed a PLSA clustering method for classifying sentiment threads in emails. Utilizing features like SWN lexicon, LDA, TF-IDF, and BoW, PLSA enabled temporal sentiment clustering and thread polarity classification. The model's performance was assessed using F1-score, accuracy, recall, and precision.

In 2020, Murugavel and Santhi [79] focused on spam filtering to reduce junk email. By verifying spam against a corpus and using spam keywords, their algorithm effectively identified diverse spam threads, providing robust solutions against ethical hacking.

In 2012, Carlos and Francine [93] developed a PCA-based spam email classifier, reducing principal components for efficient filtering. The PCADR model, tested with simulations, surpassed conventional SVM in performance for classifying junk and phishing emails.

In 2005, Zorkadis et al. [92] suggested an information-theoretic spam detection approach, minimizing false negatives and positives with FN and FP filters. The model, combining ADTree and Random Committee filters, outperformed existing methods in classification performance on standard datasets.

In 2018, Bahgat et al. [91] proposed a semantic-based spam filtering model. Using WordNet, PCA, and CFS to reduce feature dimensions, this method minimized computational costs while enhancing accuracy, as demonstrated on the Enron dataset.

2.7 Unaddressed Challenges

Deep learning and machine learning methods are widely used in spam filtering, with the ability to distinguish various characteristics of email content. However, these methods face several critical challenges:

- They lack sufficient accessibility and reliability in data, which hinders training performance due to data scarcity.
- They are often unsuitable for real-world scenarios such as spam connections, malicious activities, credit card fraud, and financial fraud.
- Regular retraining is required, but new instances of unwanted behavior complicate maintaining consistent system updates.
- Their effectiveness in maintaining integrity in spam detection is limited.
- Current machine learning algorithms are hampered by high computational costs and issues with dimensionality.
- They struggle to detect targeted, exploratory, causative, and indiscriminate attacks. Handling the concept drift phenomenon in email spam detection remains challenging.
- They are adept at identifying and classifying spam in text form, yet struggle with spam embedded in images—a tactic used by sophisticated spammers.
- Additional strategies are needed to improve reconfigurability, real-time processing, classification, and reduce power consumption.
- Existing learning-based spam detection approaches make accurate classification decisions challenging.
- Overall, these machine and deep learning spam detection systems lack robustness.

This chapter discusses traditional machine learning and deep learning methods for email spam detection, as well as optimization algorithms and clustering techniques applied to identify spam. Additionally, it highlights the research gaps and challenges in conventional spam detection approaches, providing insights that could assist researchers in advancing email spam detection.

CHAPTER

3

Email Spam Detection Approach I

3.1 Introduction

This chapter deals with the fitness oriented levy improvement-based dragonfly algorithm, an improved email spam detection deep learning approach. Email has become essential in our daily lives, making online communication increasingly crucial in today's world. However, spam emails pose a significant challenge, as they consume substantial bandwidth and storage. Consequently, filtering spam to prevent the misclassification of legitimate emails has become one of the internet's biggest challenges. This paper presents a method for detecting spam emails to strengthen cybersecurity. Initially, datasets containing text and images are gathered from various sources to identify spam emails. Feature extraction is performed on visual and textual data, with text features identified using TF-IDF, while visual features are extracted through a gray level co-occurrence matrix (GLCM) and color correlograms. Optimal features are then selected using FLI-DA. Following feature selection, spam detection is performed using a hybrid learning method, which combines two deep learning models, RNNs and CNNs. Ultimately, the collected data is classified as spam or ham through RNNs and CNNs, making this proposed approach effective in categorizing spam emails using advanced deep learning techniques.

3.2 Architecture of the FLI-DA Email Spam Detection Technique

Email is one of the most reliable and essential forms of financial communication. With an increasing number of users, the volume of spam emails has also

DOI: 10.1201/9788743810384-3

risen. Automatic classification methods, such as text mining, are used to categorize spam emails. Various deep learning and machine learning approaches have been developed by researchers to detect spam in emails, including techniques like artificial immune systems, naïve Bayes (NB), deep neural networks (DNNs), neural networks (NNs), k-nearest neighbor (K-NN), and support vector machines (SVMs). However, these methods have not fully resolved the issue of complexity. Figure 3.1 presents the structure of an improved spam email detection framework using deep learning.

In the data collection phase, emails are gathered from four different datasets, with one dataset containing images and the other three containing text. The next phase involves feature extraction, where text features are derived from the text datasets, and visual features from the image dataset. Text features are analyzed using TF-IDF to identify spam-related words, while color correlograms and GLCM are used to extract visual features. The dataset is then divided into training and testing subsets, with a total of twenty optimal features selected. CNN and RNN deep learning models are utilized for final detection.

Figure 3.1: The implemented architecture of email spam detection using a deep learning algorithm for cybersecurity.

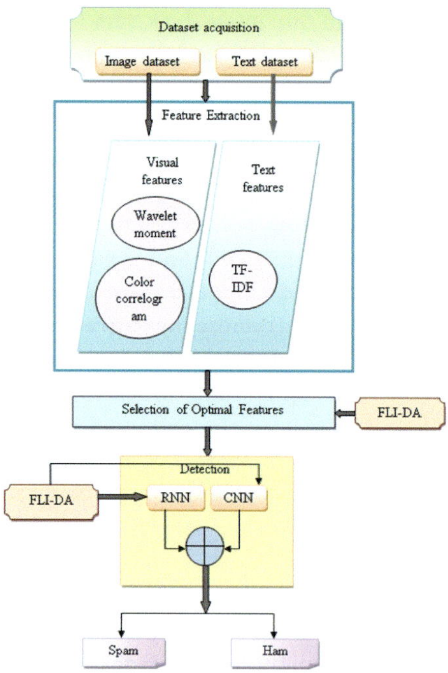

To improve the effectiveness of the proposed spam detection system, FLI-DA is used to tune the hidden neurons in both CNNs and RNNs.

3.3 Dataset Description

The necessary emails are collected from various datasets sourced from different databases. Four distinct types of datasets are utilized: one dataset contains image features, while the remaining three are text-based.

- **Dataset 1**: The Ling-spam dataset, the first text dataset, contains 2893 spam and non-spam messages and is referenced from [98]. Primarily focused on job postings and research opportunities, it has been filtered to exclude header information related to research. It includes 2412 legitimate messages and 481 spam messages.
- **Dataset 2**: The second text dataset is the spam mail dataset, sourced from [99]. This dataset includes both ham and spam emails and contains an "enron1" folder with numerous emails across various folders.
- **Dataset 3**: Named the spam-or-ham-email classification dataset, the third text dataset, sourced from [100], comprises 2371 tasks and a total of 71,325 datasets.
- **Dataset 4**: The fourth dataset is the image spam dataset, referenced from [101]. This dataset includes emails collected directly from actual users.

3.4 Extraction of Text Features using TF-IDF

Text features are extracted from the text datasets. TF-IDF is used to identify the number of spam words, while the corpus manages word frequency by filtering out some high-importance words. Due to TF-IDF's simplicity, comparing documents is straightforward. TF-IDF flags all suspicious documents.

The formula for text feature extraction is given in Eq. (3.1), where TF (represented as TXF) denotes frequency:

$$TXF_{b,a} = \frac{p_{b,a}}{\sum_{k=0}^{j} p_{k,a}} \tag{3.1}$$

Here, $p_{b,a}$ defines the number of occurrences of the bth word in a document Qa. The denominator defines the total number of words in the document Qa . IDF is denoted by *Idfx*, and IDF is calculated by using Eq. (3.2).

$$Idfx = \log\left(\frac{|Q|}{|\{g_a \in Q : n_b \in g_1\}|}\right) \tag{3.2}$$

The term Q defines the number of documents in the corpus and $\{g_a \in Q : n_b \in g_1\}$ denotes the number of documents in the attributes *nb*. The formula *TXF – Idf* is described in Eq. (3.3).

$$TXF - Idf = TXF * Idfx = \frac{P_{b,a}}{\sum_{k=0}^{j} p_{k,a}} * \log\left(\frac{|Q|}{|\{g_a \in Q : n_b \in g_1\}|}\right) \quad (3.3)$$

When the number of documents in the corpus increases, the inverse document frequency (IDF) value decreases. If the text's distinguishing characteristics are minimal, dynamic attributes become more prominent, resulting in equal weighting across all corpus documents. To counter this effect, a value is added to the denominator. High-frequency terms are generally less significant, while lower-frequency terms are often more meaningful, providing richer features.

The extracted term reflects the specific textual features identified, leading to a total of 600 textual features. The term H_{cf}^{txt} is the extracted textual feature, where $cf = 1,2,\cdots,CF$. CF indicates the retrieved textual features.

3.5 Extraction of Visual Features using a GLCM and a Color Correlogram

3.5.1 Visual feature extraction

In email spam detection, visual features are extracted from image datasets using a gray level co-occurrence matrix (GLCM) and color correlogram methods.

GLCM: Image features are derived through GLCM by analyzing statistically similar intensity values distributed throughout the image. Points within the image are categorized into first, second, and higher-order statistics based on potential image points. Although higher-order statistics yield theoretical insights, they are computationally demanding. GLCM texture characteristics capture information on surface structure and pixel relationships, allowing for straightforward implementation with strong results.

3.5.2 Texture-oriented features

Energy: Also known as "angular second moment" or "uniformity," this feature measures pixel uniformity. The GLCM matrix calculates it by summing squared elements, moving from varied regions to more uniform ones. Thus, repetitive pixels appear more frequently, and the energy value rises, as per Eq. (3.4).

$$Eng = \sum_{ky,ly=0}^{Oy-1} (Rs_{kyly})^2 \tag{3.4}$$

Entropy: Entropy measures the randomness or unpredictability within an image. For more uniform (homogeneous) images, entropy tends to yield lower values. The calculation formula for entropy is shown in Eq. (3.5).

$$Ent = \sum_{ky,ly=0}^{Oy-1} -\ln(Rs_{kyly})\, Rs_{kyly} \tag{3.5}$$

Contrast: Contrast evaluates the intensity difference between a pixel and its neighboring pixels. It quantifies the strength of these differences within the image, as represented in Eq. (3.6).

$$Con = \sum_{ky,ly=0}^{Oy-1} Rs_{kyly}(ky - ly)^2 \tag{3.6}$$

Correlation: Correlation assesses the linear relationship between pixel intensities in an image. It examines the gray tones to define the association between pixels, as represented by the formula in Eq. (3.7).

$$Cor = \sum_{ky,ly=0}^{Oy-1} Rs_{kyly} \frac{(ky - \lambda)(ly - \lambda)}{\alpha^2} \tag{3.7}$$

Homogeneity: Homogeneity measures the degree of similarity between pixels. Within the GLCM (gray level co-occurrence matrix), higher values indicate more uniform textures, minimizing the need for texture adjustment. The formula is provided in Eq. (3.8).

$$Hom = \sum_{ky,lyz=0}^{Oy-1} \frac{Rs_{kyly}}{1 + (ky - ly)^2} \tag{3.8}$$

The above equations include elements from the normalized GLCM matrix, and the mean of these values is shown in Eq. (3.9).

$$\lambda = \sum_{ky,ly=0}^{Oy-1} kyRs_{kyly} \tag{3.9}$$

Variance: The intensity variance, or distribution of pixel intensities, is calculated for each pixel, where the total number of gray levels in the image is also considered.

A variance of intensities of every pixel is denoted by α. It is shown in Eq. (3.10).

$$\alpha^2 = \sum_{ky,ly=0}^{Oy-1} Rs_{kyly}(ky - \mu)^2 \tag{3.10}$$

Here, the number of gray levels in the picture is represented by *Oy*.

Color correlogram: Color correlograms are typically used as feature vectors for pictures. A color histogram shows the image's overall color distribution. Tiny changes in the screening positions have no effect on the calculation, which is easier. This is vulnerable even though it primarily concentrates on false positives and does not have spatial data for the large databases. Furthermore, notable appearances have no effect on the histogram. These limitations are addressed by the color correlogram. Minimal dimensionality is used to represent the textures that were retrieved. Very large visual changes in the scene can be corrected by the color correlogram. The following details explain how the auto color correlogram works:

- First, the input image undergoes 64 -color quantization. The colors of the provided spam or ham images are categorized into color values $C_1, C_2, C_3, \cdots C_{64}$.
- For each pixel, a neighborhood 3×3 is taken into account based on the distance d. The original color correlogram is used as the basis for determining the distance $d = 1, 3, 4$ and 7 . It is possible to distinguish the center pixel's value from all eight pixels in a neighborhood. The local spatial distribution of the pixels is described by the probability of the pixel count. The terms s_1 and s_2 are pixels, color is represented as C_i, the image is described as ime and distance is denoted as d. Choosing the alternative pixel is given in Eq. (3.11).

$$\gamma^d C_l(ime) = Rtnc\,ncl\,[|s_1 - s_2| = d, s_2 \in ime\,C_l \mid s_1 \in ime\,C_{.l}\,|] \tag{3.11}$$

- Within this instance, this probability exists for every single pixel. It creates a 64-dimensional feature vector when used as a visual feature vector.

Color correlograms and the GLCM have been combined to create a total of 3537 visual features. Consequently, the count of visual features that are obtained using color correlograms and the GLCM is defined as follows: $H^{vis} = \{GCLM, \text{color correlogram}\}$here,

$ct = 1, 2, \cdots, CT \qquad ct^*$ where

The final visual features extracted are defined as *CT*.

3.6 Selection of Optimal Features

Choosing the best features aims to minimize the quantity of inputs required for additional processing and analysis. This is also employed to identify the most relevant inputs. In this instance, the optimal feature selection is achieved with the aid of a novel meta-heuristic algorithm called FLI-DA. A total of 600 textual features are fully realized. The term $H_{cf^*}^{txt^*}$ refers to textual features that have been optimally selected. Where $cf^* = 1, 2, \cdots, CF^*$. CF^* indicates the number of optimally selected textual features, which is equal to 20. Similarly, a total of 3537 visual features were obtained. Visual features that are optimally chosen are represented by the term $H_{ct^*}^{vis^*}$ where $ct^* = 1, 2, \cdots, CT^*$. Where CT^* represents optimally chosen image features.

Optimal Feature Selection and Classification Using the Levy Improvement-based Dragonfly Algorithm

Objective function: The primary aim of the proposed email spam detection method utilizing a deep learning algorithm is to attain a high detection accuracy rate. The employed FLI-DA is utilized to optimize the hidden neurons of both the CNN and RNN and to choose the most effective features. CNN and RNN are employed to identify spam in emails. The calculation of the objective function is presented in Eq. (3.12).

$$Ofn = \underset{\{G_{ps}, I_{CNN}, I_{RNN}\}}{\text{argmax}} (Ay) \tag{3.12}$$

Here *Ofn* denotes an objective function *Gps* and specifies the chosen features optimally, here, $ps = 1, 2, \cdots, PS$. Here, PS signifies the complete count of features.

The optimized hiddenneurons available in CNNs are represented by the term *ICNN*. Likewise, hidden neurons in RNN are expressed by *IRNN*, and accuracy is indicated as *Ay*. The equation for accuracy is detailed in Eq. (3.13).

$$Ay = \frac{TEPS + TENG}{TEPS + TENG + FEPS + FENG} \tag{3.13}$$

Figure 3.2: Encoded solution. Conventional Dragonfly Algorithm

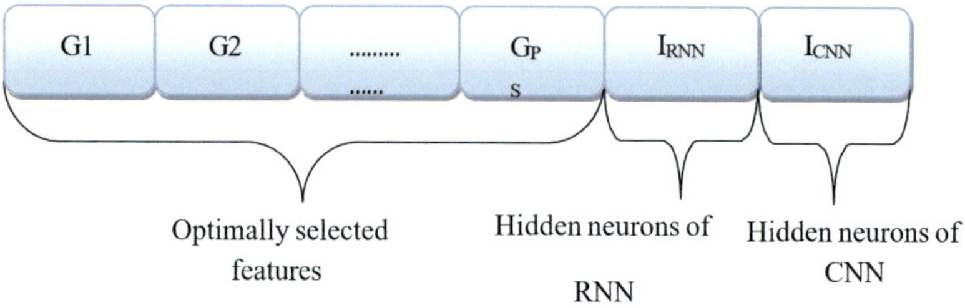

Here, a true positive is indicated as *TEPS*, a true negative is indicated as *TENG*, a false positive is indicated as *FEPS*, and a false negative is indicated as *FENG*.

Encoded solution: Figure 3.2 illustrates the encoded solution of the implemented email spam detection method. The employed FLI-DA is utilized to enhance hidden neurons in CNNs and RNNs, as well as to choose the optimal features. The bounding limit of the hidden neurons in the CNNs and RNNs is 5255. Performance is assured when each variable is fine-tuned within the bounding limit. In Figure 3.2, the features are represented as $G_1, G_2, \cdots, G_{PS}$. *PS* is defined by the number of optimally selected features, which is 20. In terms of extracting the quality of the solution, encoding requires a significant amount of time. The overall encoded solution cannot ensure the feasibility of the solution.

3.7 Conventional Dragonfly Algorithm

The dynamic and static swarming actions of dragonflies serve as a source of inspiration for the dragonfly algorithm (DA) [26]. The phases of exploration and exploitation are comparable to these swarming actions. In the exploration phase, the dragonflies chase after the remaining flying prey. During the exploitation phase, many dragonflies travel in the same direction. Consequently, all the swarms begin to advance toward the food while being diverted by adversaries. The detachment of a mth dragonfly j_m from its neighboring dragonfly is expressed in Eq. (3.14).

$$V_m = \sum_{d=1}^{Q'} \left(Y' - Y'_d\right) \tag{3.14}$$

In the above equation $Q^{'}$ denotes the number of neighboring individuals. The location of the dth neighbor is referred to as $Y_d^{'}$, and the position of individuals is represented as $Y^{'}$. Eq. (3.15) determines the alignment.

$$D_m = \frac{\sum_{d=1}^{Q'} U_d'}{Q'} \tag{3.15}$$

Here, $U_d^{'}$ is the velocity of the dth neighboring individual. Eq. (3.16) shows the formulation.

$$B_m = \frac{\sum_{d=1}^{Q'} Y'd}{Q'} - Y' \tag{3.16}$$

Eq. (3.17) computes the attracted food source

$$I_m = Fd - Y' \tag{3.17}$$

The food source's location is defined as *Fd* in the above equation. The enemy-facing diversion is calculated by Eq. (3.18).

$$J_m = Eny + Y' \tag{3.18}$$

Here, the term Eny is the enemy's position. Position Y' and step $\Delta Y'$ represent the two vectors that are utilized to replicate the movements of the dragonfly and to update their position. Equation (3.19) outlines a step vector that illustrates the direction of the traveling dragonflies.

$$\Delta Y_{a+1}' = \left(v'V_m + d'D_m + b'B_m + i'I_m + j'J_m\right) + \delta \cdot \Delta Y_a' \tag{3.19}$$

The above equation shows the iteration counter. The inertia weigh is represented by the term δ. The individual enemy's m th position is represented as J_m, enemy factor is shown by j', the m th individual food source is represented as I_m, and i_m' represents the food factor. The term B represents the cohesion of the m th individual, b' is the weight of the cohesion, D_m defines the arrangement of the m th individual, d' is the alignment weight, the separation of the m th individual is represented as V_m, and v' is the separation weight. Position vectors are calculated in Eq. (3.20).

$$Y_{a+1}' = Y_a' + \Delta Y_{a+1}' \tag{3.20}$$

Eq. (3.21), (3.22), and (3.23) are used for updating the position of dragonflies,

$$Y_{a+1}' = Y_a' + Ly(g) + Y_a' \tag{3.21}$$

$$Ly(g) = 0.01 \times \frac{sv_1 \times \delta}{|sv_2|^{\frac{1}{g}}} \tag{3.22}$$

$$\delta = \left(\frac{\Omega(1+\beta) \times \sin\left(\frac{\gamma\beta}{2}\right)}{\Omega\left(\frac{1+\beta}{2}\right) \times \beta \times 2^{\left(\frac{\beta-1}{2}\right)}} \right)^{\frac{1}{\beta}} \tag{3.23}$$

$$\Omega(y) = (y-1)! \tag{3.24}$$

Here β is a constant. The terms sv_1 and sv_2 are the two numbers that lie in between [0,1].

The term g represents the dimension of the position vectors. The term a is the current iteration. The pseudo-code for the traditional DA algorithm is given in Algorithm 3.1.

Algorithm 3.1. DA algorithm

Start up the population of dragonflies $Y_m(m-1, 2, \cdots, r)$

Configure step vectors $\Delta Y_q(m = 1, 2, \cdots, r)$

while the condition is not met

Calculate each value of dra gonflies

Updating food source and enemy

Updating j, i, b, d, and v

Calculate J, I, B, D, and V using Eq. (3.14), (3.15), (3.16), (3.17), and (3.18)

if (food's distance > radius)

  if $(R' > 1)$

    Update velocity vector using Eq. (3.19)

    Update position vector using Eq. (3.20)

else

Update position vector using Eq. (3.21)

end if

Based on variable boundaries, verify and precise upcoming positions

end while

3.8 Implementation of FLI-DA

By utilizing the recommended FLI-DA, the features are selected in an optimal manner and the hidden neurons in the RNNs and CNNs are tuned. Without any human involvement, CNNs can quickly identify the essential features. CNNs function as an effective dense network that carries out both identification and prediction tasks. The precision of CNNs is elevated when provided with high-quality data. By the time the data is retrieved, the time series can also be easily predicted through RNNs. RNNs have the capability to process input of any length. Although the input size may be large, the model size does not surpass it. Expert systems and decision-making systems are developed using optimization principles. The primary elements impacting the optimization algorithms are classification and prediction performance. The levy flight. According to Eq. (3.25), if $(f_m > \text{mean}\,(f_m))$ then the solution is $U = ghr\,(Y' - Eny)$. The position vector is determined using Eq. (3.25).

$$Y'_{a+1} = Y' + hU \tag{3.25}$$

Or else, if $ft_m \leq \text{mean}\,(ft_m)$, then the solution is updated as $X = ghr\,(Y' - Fd)$ and computation of the position vector is described in Eq. (3.26).

$$Y'_{a+1} = Y' + hX \tag{3.26}$$

Here, *h* represents a random number, and it lies between -1, -1. Figure 3.3 shows the flowchart of the suggested FLI-DA. Algorithm 3.2 illustrates the pseudocode of the executed FLI-DA.

Algorithm 3.2. Algorithm for implemented FLI-DA

Start up the population of dragonflies $r_m(m = 1, 2 \cdots r)$,

Configure step vectors by $\Delta Y_m(w = 1, 2, \cdots r)$,

While the condition does not meet the extend

Calculate each value of dragonflies

Updating food source and enemy

Updating j, b, b, d, and v

Calculate J, A, B, D, and V using Eq. (3.14), Eq. (3.15), Eq. (3.16), Eq. (3.17), and Eq. (3.18)

if (food's distance > radius)

if $(R' > 1)$

Update velocity vector using Eq. (3.19)

Update position vector using Eq. (3.20)

else

if $(ft_m > meder\,(ft_m))$

Update position vector using Eq. (3.25)

else

Update position vector using Eq. (3.26)

end if

Based on variable boundaries, verify and precise upcoming positions

end while

Figure 3.3: Flowchart of the implemented FLI-DA.

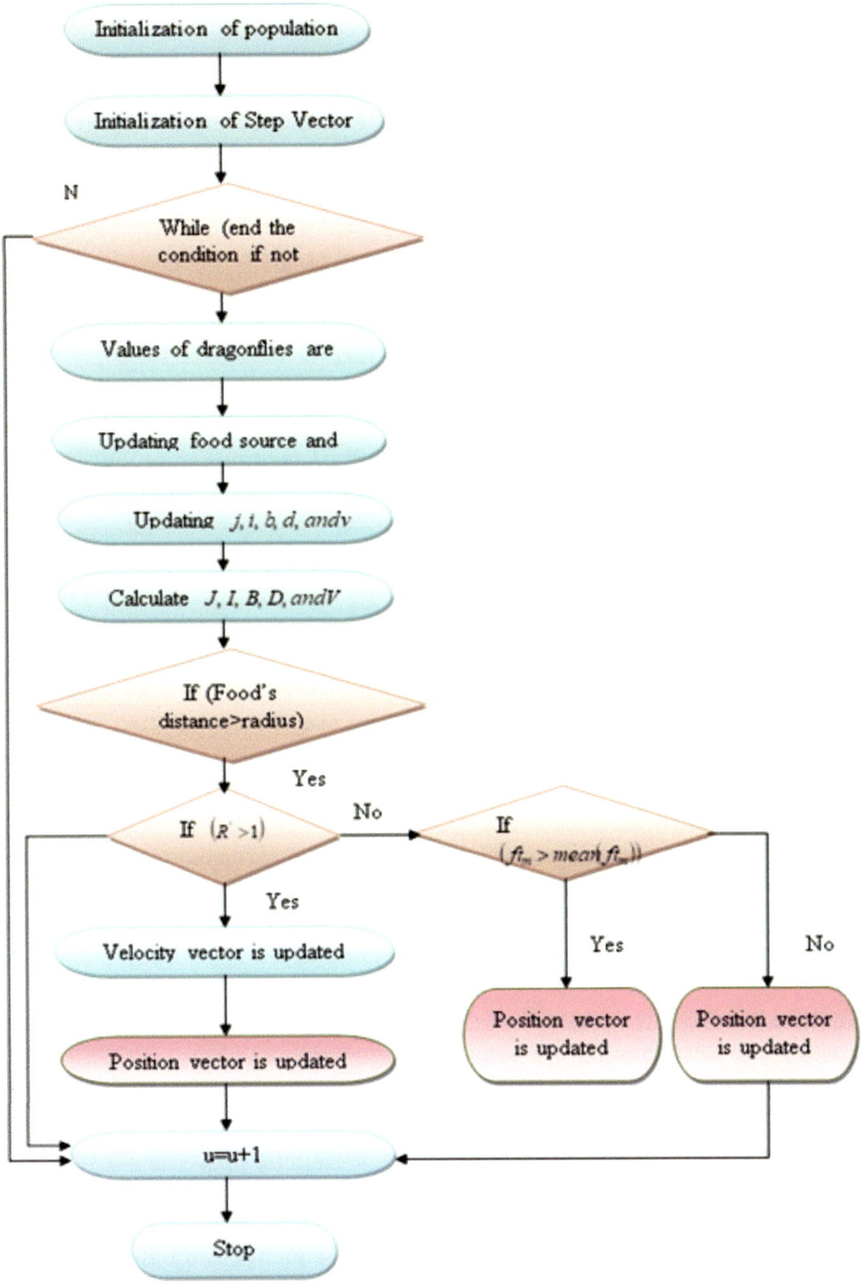

3.9 Classification of Image and Text Features using a Hybrid Model

Document images are classified through visual and textual attributes. Utilizing word similarity, textual attributes successfully convey emotional semantics. Furthermore, the analysis of texts is employed to uncover the values within the texts that correspond to the test images. The visual attributes provide a thorough description of this content.

Convolutional neural network: CNNs [110] consist of two components. Pooling and convolution operations are utilized in part 1 to generate the deep features of the raw data. In part 2, these features are linked to an MLP for classification purposes. Below is an explanation of each layer.

Input layer: The scope of each univariate series is specified *N*, and the number of input times is mentioned. Both consist of $N \times t$ neurons. The input layer of the neural network model is designed to accept the training images.

Convolutional layer: Convolution operations are carried out on the preceding time series layer utilizing the convolution filters. The nonlinear transformation function is known as ntf . The convolution operation retrieves the fc time series. The range of each univariate is specified as $\Gamma_N{}^{-1} + 7$ and the time series is denoted as $_t$, and N defines the range of each $^{\mathrm{L}uv1}$ univariate. In this scenario, rounding down is defined as $\lfloor . \rfloor$. Through the use of a convolution layer, the necessary features are extracted by reducing the parameters. It presents the concept of generalization and mitigates the issue of over-fitting.

Pooling layer: The feature map is separated into *N* equal segments. Additionally, the highest or average value of each segment is utilized to recognize each segment. The pooling layer serves to minimize the overhead linked to dataset security. Every hidden layer includes the pooling layer.

Feature layer: Several feature maps represent the real-time during different pooling and convolution processes.

Output layer: The output layer is composed of *ns* neurons associated with *ns* class time. In function-fitting scenarios, the linear output layer is consistently employed.

CNN training: The CNN model is trained using a sequence of training examples $((x, y_1), (x_2, y_2), \cdots, (x_{N\text{ sample}}, y_{N\text{ sample}}))$ having $x_v \in \Re^{N \times l}, y_v \in \Re^n$ for $1 \leq v \leq N$ sample. The resultant output is a vector y_v, and the input can be either a multivariate or univariate time series x_v. The network training involves the following steps:

Step 1: A small random value acts as the foundation for initializing the weights and bias. Eq. (3.27) offers the subsequent descriptions of an activation function, *bh*, with the sigmoid function denoted as *sig*.

$$bh(u) = sig(u) = \frac{1}{1+e^{-u}} \tag{3.27}$$

Step 2: From a training set, a training sample is chosen randomly.

Step 3: The convolutional layer's output is shown in Eq. (3.28).

$$JK_t(v) = \text{bh}\left(\sum_{q=1}^{m}\sum_{p=1}^{d} x(q+et(v-1),p)rs_t(q,p)+ct(t)\right) \tag{3.28}$$

In the above equation, the bias and weight of the t th convolution filters are denoted as $ct(t)$ and $r_{S_t \in \Re^{m\times d}}$ the vth component of the tth feature map is represented as $JK_t(v)$.et is represented as a convolution stride, and the input or output time series is denoted as $u \in \Re^{N\times d}$. The output of the pooling layer is computed using Eq. (3.29).

$$BL_t(v) = f\left(JK_t((v-1)mn+1), JL_t((v-1)mn+2), \cdots, JK_t(vmn)\right) \tag{3.29}$$

Here, the term f defines the pooling strategy and BL defines the pooling layer. The result of the output layer is described in Eq. (3.30).

$$OT(p) = bh\left(\sum_{q=1}^{N} y(q)rs_{bh}(q,p)+ct_{bh}(p)\right), \quad p = 1,2,\cdots,ns \tag{3.30}$$

Here, the feature layer and connection weights are represented as $rs_{bh} \in \Re^{\times ns} \cdot ct_{bh}$ is the bias of the output layer and the feature map is denoted by y . The mean-square error is defined in Eq. (3.31).

$$EO = \frac{1}{2}\sum_{d=1}^{ns} h(d)^2 = \frac{1}{2}\sum_{d=1}^{ns}(OT(d)-y(d))^2 \tag{3.31}$$

Step 4: The bias and weights are updated using the gradient descent method, which is shown in Eq. (3.32).

$$g = g - \xi\frac{\varphi EO}{\varphi g} \tag{3.32}$$

In the above equation, ct_{bh}, ct, rs_{bh} and rs_t are denoted by the parameter value g.

Step 5: Repeat step 3 until all the samples are trained with the training set.

Step 6: Once the iteration count reaches the maximum value, the algorithm stops. Or else it moves to step 2.

Figure 3.4: Hybrid classifier to detect spam in email.

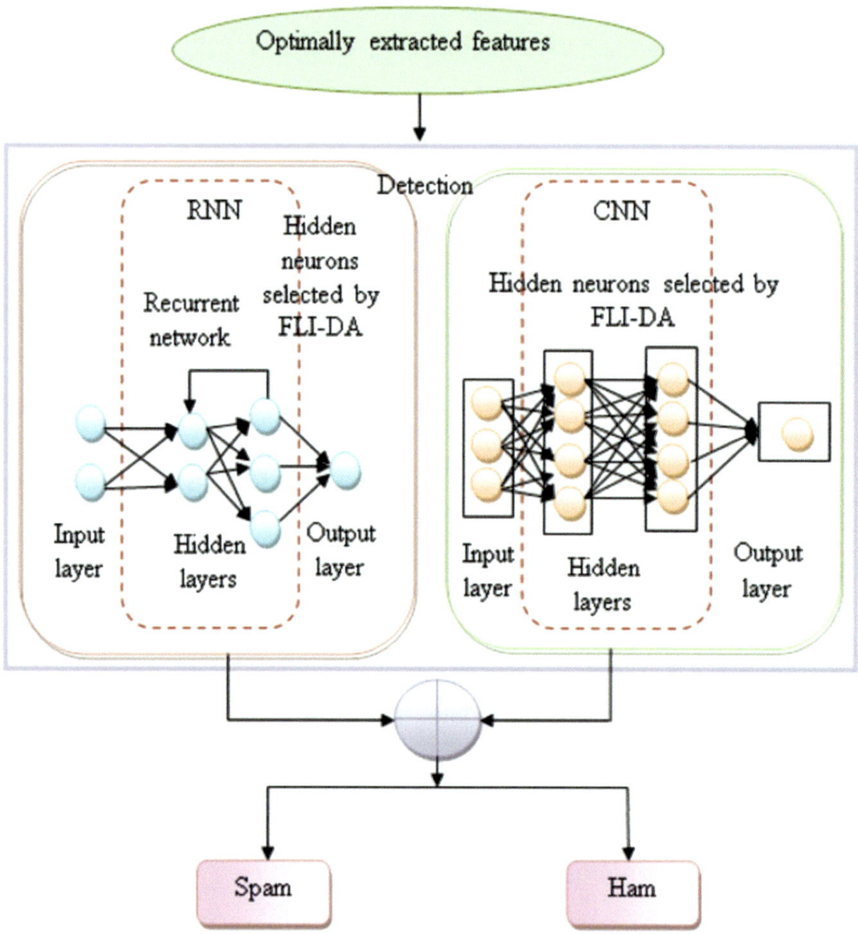

Recurrent neural network: One of the distributions of artificial neural networks is the recurrent neural network, denoted as RNN [103]. The gated recurrent unit is a specific type of long short-term memory. The usage of GRU simplifies the RNN. A single gate is formed from the output gates, functioning as an update gate u. The current state is obtained via linear interpolation. The main benefits consist of reduced parameters and easier training processes. The mtth image slice's input features are (y, q). Eq. (3.33) and Eq. (3.34) talk about the update gate u and reset gate r.

$$u_{mt} = \varepsilon \left(X^{yu} y_{mt} + X^{qu} q_{mt-1} \right) \tag{3.33}$$

$$r_{mt} = \varepsilon \left(X^{yr} y_{mt} + X^{qr} q_{mt-1} \right) \tag{3.34}$$

The term ε represents the logistic sigmoid function. X^{yu}, X^{qu}, X^{yr} and X^{qr} are the weight matrices. The hidden unit is computed from Eq. (3.35).

$$\tilde{q}_{mt} = \tan \left(X^{yq} y_{mt} + X^{qq} \left(q_{mt-1} \Gamma r_{mt} \right) \right) \tag{3.35}$$

Here, Γ represents the element-wise multiplication. The mt th hidden activation state of q_{nt} the candidate's earlier state is referred to as $\tilde{q}_{mt}$, and q_{mt-1} which is shown in Eq. (3.36).

$$q_{mt} = \left(1 - u_{mt}\right) \Gamma \tilde{q}_{mt} + u_{mt} \Gamma q_{mt-1} q_{mt} = \left(1 - u_{mt}\right) \Gamma \tilde{q}_{mt} + u_{mt} \Gamma q_{mt-1} \tag{3.36}$$

Hybridization of two classifiers: A hybrid classifier combining RNNs and CNNs is employed in the detection stage following the selection of the optimal features. As a consequence, the hidden neurons are fine-tuned. The bit operations from RNN and CNN are utilized to ascertain whether the data is classified as spam or ham. The diagrammatical representation of the hybrid classifier is shown in Figure 3.4.

CHAPTER

4

Performance Analysis of FLI-DA

4.1 Experimental Setup and Parameter Settings

The developed deep learning-enabled email spam identification approach was implemented in Python version 3.7. The system had 8 gigabytes of random access memory. Python was employed to implement the proposed detection of spam in email, with the subsequent results being analyzed. A population of ten people was involved, and a total of 25 iterations were conducted. Four datasets were used, with the first three mirroring the textual format and the fourth dataset mirroring the image. The proposed FLI-DA-CRNN method's performance was evaluated by comparing its experimental results against established methods including DA-CRNN [102], GWO-CRNN [105], PSO-CRNN [104] and WOA-CRNN [106]. For the analysis of performance on the developed model, deep learning techniques including RNN [103], CNN [110], and CRNN [110] [103] were used. Machine learning models like SVM [109], NN [111], DT [108], and KNN [110] were also used.

4.1.1 Parameter settings

Table 4.1 illustrates the experimental parameters employed in the development of a deep learning- based approach for detecting email spam.

DOI: 10.1201/9788743810384-4

Table 4.1: Experimental parameters

Methods	DA [102]	PSO [104]	WOA [106]
Experimental parameters	Fitness of food = 'inf. 'Fitness of enemy = 'inf.'	wmin = 0.1; wmax = 0.9; c1 = 2; c2 = 2;	A score of the Leader = ' inf.'

4.2 Performance Analysis of FLI-DA in Terms of Accuracy with Different Optimization Algorithms

The performance of the proposed FLI-DA-CRNN-based email spam detection model was evaluated across four datasets, depicted in Figure 4.1. According to Figure 4.1 (a), the proposed FLI-DA-CRNN outperformed PSO-CRNN by 6.08%, GWO-CRNN by 4.52%, WOA-CRNN by 6.56%, and DA-CRNN by 3.93% for Dataset 1 when the learning rate was set at 85%. In Figure 4.1 (b), the accuracy of the proposed FLI-DA-CRNN-based email spam detection model outperforms PSO-CRNN by 3.42%, GWO-CRNN by 2.95%, WOA-CRNN by 2.02%, and DA-CRNN by 1.45% in Dataset 2 under a 75% learning rate. In Figure 4.1 (c), The proposed FLI-DA-CRNN-based email spam detection model achieves enhanced accuracy of 2.67% more than the GWO-CRNN, 4.64% more than the PSO-CRNN, 5.36% more than the DA-CRNN, and 3.24% more than the WOA-CRNN in Dataset 3. The accuracy of the proposed FLI-DA-CRNN-based email spam detection model in Figure 4.1 (d) is 2.15% greater than DA-CRNN, 3.32% greater than WOA-CRNN, 2.03% greater than GWO-CRNN, and 3.2% greater than PSO-CRNN when trained on Dataset 4 at an 85% learning rate. The conclusion can be drawn that the proposed FLI-DA-CRNN performs better than several other established optimization models.

4.3 Performance Analysis of FLI-DA using Different Machine Learning and Deep Learning Models

The performance of the proposed FLI-DA-CRNN-based email spam detection model was evaluated across four datasets, as depicted in Figure 4.2. Figure 4.2 (a) shows that the FLI-DA- CRNN-based email spam detection model achieves higher accuracy than NN, SVM, KNN, and DT, with improvements of 4.76% over NN, 8.64% over SVM, 7.32% over KNN, and 6.02% over DT, when the learning percentage is set to 75% for Dataset 1. The FLI-DA-CRNN-based email spam detection model exhibited a higher accuracy than NN by 12.5%, KNN by 8.43%, DT by 9.76%, and SVM by 9.76%, shown in Figure 4.2 (b), specifically with an 85% learning rate within Dataset 2. As shown in Figure 4.2 (c), FLI-DA-CRNN

Figure 4.1: Comparative performance analysis of the proposed email spam detection using deep learning for Datasets 1, 2, 3, and 4 relative to existing prior works.

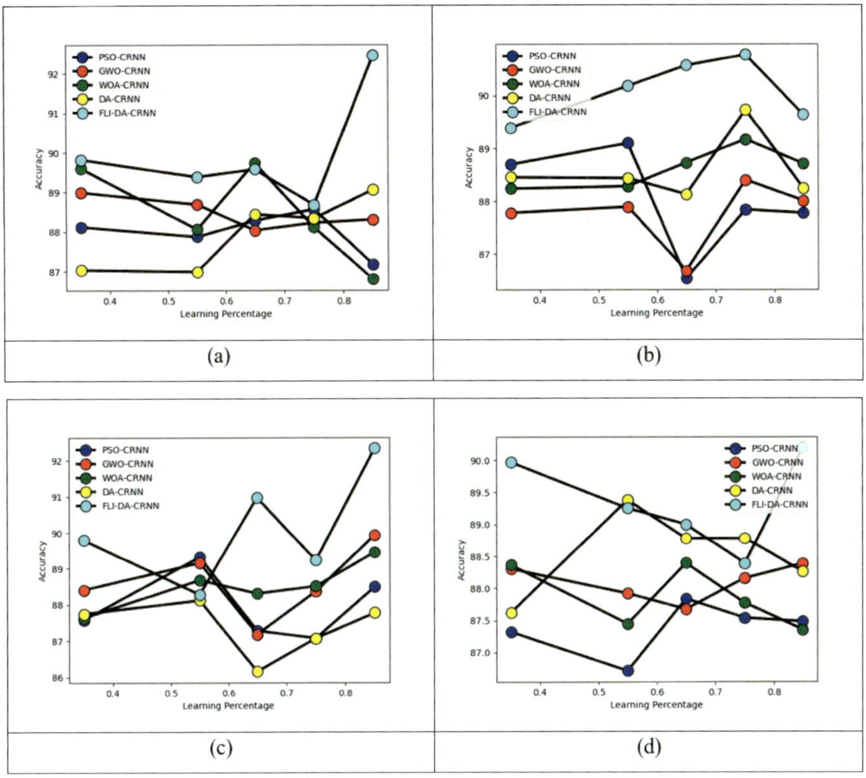

surpasses NN by 9.76%, SVM by 8.43%, KNN by 9.76%, and DT by 7.14% when a learning rate of 75% is applied to Dataset 3. Figure 4.2 (d) shows that the FLI-DA-CRNN-based email spam detection model outperforms NN by 4.88%, SVM by 6.17%, KNN by 7.5%, and DT by 3.61% in Dataset 4, with a 75% learning rate. The results indicate that the implementation of the FLI-DA-CRNN-based model for detecting spam in emails yields more effective outcomes compared to alternative machine learning approaches.

Figures 4.2 (e)–(h) demonstrate that the proposed FLI-DA-CRNN–based email spam detection model achieves greater accuracy than the conventional CNN, RNN, and CRNN architectures across Datasets 1 through 4. For each dataset, the accuracy curve of the FLI-DA-CRNN model exceeds that of the baseline models, indicating improved feature extraction, better learning capability,

Figure 4.2: Continued.

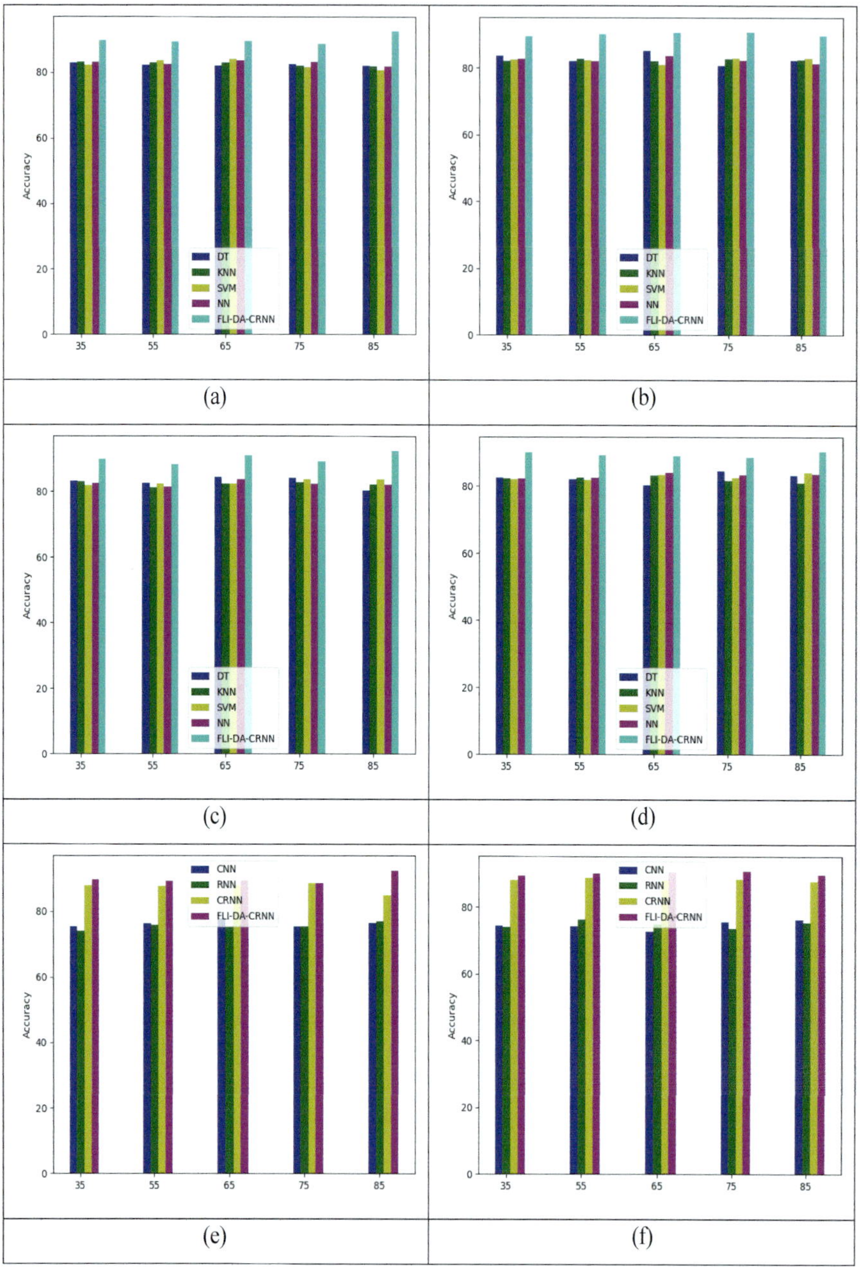

Figure 4.2: Analyzing the accuracy of developed spam detection using machine learning and deep learning algorithms among the Datasets 1, 2, 3 and 4

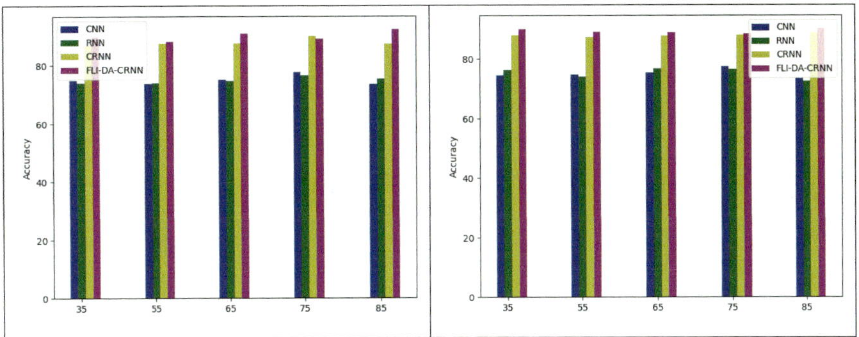

(g) (h)

and enhanced classification performance. These results validate the robustness and effectiveness of the proposed framework.

4.4 Performance Analysis of the Proposed FLI-DA-CRNN Email Spam Detection Model

An analysis was conducted on the efficacy of the proposed FLI-DA-CRNN-based email spam detection model using four datasets. The effectiveness of the proposed model is summarized in Tables 4.2, 4.3, and 4.4. The email spam detection model proposed, based on FLI- DA-CRNN, outperforms the GWO-CRNN model by 4.70%, the PSO-CRNN model by 6.06%, the DA-CRNN model by 3.81%, and the WOA-CRNN model by 6.52% in Dataset 1 as shown in Table 4.1. According to Table 4.4, for Dataset 2, the FLI-DA-CRNN model achieved a higher accuracy than CRNN by 2.26%, RNN by 18.83%, and CNN by 17.38%. In addition, Table 4.3 indicates that, for Dataset 3, FLI-DA-CRNN yielded a higher accuracy than KNN by 12.24%, SVM by 10.32%, NN by 12.24%, and DT by 14.93%. The FLI-DA-CRNN also demonstrated a higher accuracy of 7.37% compared to SVM, 8.54% compared to DT, 7.87% compared to NN, and 11.48% compared to KNN for Dataset 4. The findings demonstrate a significant enhancement in spam detection in email using the proposed FLI-DA-CRNN approach.

Table 4.2: Performance analysis of detecting spam emails using improved deep learning algorithms for cyber security with four different types of datasets.

Dataset 1										
Techniques	Accuracy	FPR	NPV	FDR	Sensitivity	MCC	F1-score	FNR	Specificity	Precision
DA- CRNN [102]	0.8905 66	0.114 286	0.885 714	0.019 139	0.891 304	0.6444 1	0.933 941	0.108 696	0.8857 14	0.9808 61
WOA- CRNN [106]	0.8679 25	0.157 143	0.842 857	0.026 699	0.871 739	0.5815 66	0.919 725	0.128 261	0.8428 57	0.9733 01
GWO- CRNN [105]	0.8830 19	0.114 286	0.885 714	0.019 324	0.882 609	0.6291 33	0.929 062	0.117 391	0.8857 14	0.9806 76
PSO- CRNN [104]	0.8716 98	0.071 429	0.928 571	0.012 438	0.863 043	0.6262 16	0.921 114	0.136 957	0.9285 71	0.9875 62
FLI- DA- CRNN	0.9245 28	0.042 857	0.957 143	0.007 042	0.919 565	0.7474 14	0.954 853	0.080 435	0.9571 43	0.9929 58

Dataset 2										
Techniques	FDR	MCC	NPV	Sensitivity	FNR	Precision	F1-score	FPR	Accuracy	Specificity
DA- CRNN [102]	0.3143 94	0.716 701	0.874 242	0.909 548	0.090 452	0.6856 06	0.781 857	0.125 758	0.8824 21	0.8742 42
PSO- CRNN [104]	0.2991 45	0.680 474	0.893 939	0.824 121	0.175 879	0.7008 55	0.757 506	0.106 061	0.8777 65	0.8939 39
WOA- CRNN [106]	0.2992 13	0.720 477	0.884 848	0.894 472	0.105 528	0.7007 87	0.785 872	0.115 152	0.8870 78	0.8848 48
GWO- CRNN [105]	0.3110 24	0.702 338	0.880 303	0.879 397	0.120 603	0.6889 76	0.772 627	0.119 697	0.8800 93	0.8803 03
FLI- DA- CRNN	0.2764 23	0.738 618	0.896 97	0.894 472	0.105 528	0.7235 77	0.8	0.103 03	0.8963 91	0.8969 7

Table 4.2: Continued.

Dataset 3										
Techniques	MCC	FDR	Precision	Accuracy	Sensitivity	Specificity	FNR	NPV	EPR	F1-score
WOA- CRNN [106]	0.6458 93	0.404 762	0.595 238	0.894 484	0.833 333	0.9047 62	0.166 667	0.904 762	0.0952 38	0.6944 44
DA- CRNN [102]	0.6314 09	0.453 608	0.546 392	0.877 698	0.883 333	0.8767 51	0.116 667	0.876 751	0.1232 49	0.6751 59
GWO- CRNN [105]	0.6881 42	0.402 174	0.597 826	0.899 281	0.916 667	0.8963 59	0.083 333	0.896 359	0.1036 41	0.7236 84
PSO- CRNN [104]	0.6387 1	0.434 783	0.565 217	0.884 892	0.866 667	0.8879 55	0.133 333	0.887 955	0.1120 45	0.6842 11
FLI- DA- CRNN	0.7591 9	0.340 909	0.659 091	0.923 261	0.966 667	0.9159 66	0.033 333	0.915 966	0.0840 34	0.7837 84
Dataset 4										
Techniques	**Specificity**	**NPV**	**FNR**	**FPR**	**Accuracy**	**Precision**	**MCC**	**FDR**	**F1-score**	**Sensitivity**
WOA- CRNN [106]	0.8611 6	0.861 16	0.092 233	0.138 84	0.873 548	0.7030 08	0.715 443	0.296 992	0.7923 73	0.9077 67
PSO- CRNN [104]	0.8804 92	0.880 492	0.140 777	0.119 508	0.874 839	0.7224 49	0.702 803	0.277 551	0.7849 22	0.8592 23
DA- CRNN [102]	0.8822 5	0.882 25	0.116 505	0.117 75	0.882 581	0.7309 24	0.724 405	0.269 076	0.8	0.8834 95
GWO- CRNN [105]	0.8910 37	0.891 037	0.135 922	0.108 963	0.883 871	0.7416 67	0.721 473	0.258 333	0.7982 06	0.8640 78
FLI- DA- CRNN	0.9033 39	0.903 339	0.101 942	0.096 661	0.901 935	0.7708 33	0.765 694	0.229 167	0.8295 96	0.8980 58

Table 4.3: Performance analysis of email spam detection using improved deep learning algorithms for cyber security among various deep learning techniques.

					Dataset 1					
Techniques	**Accuracy**	**FPR**	**NPV**	**FDR**	**Sensitivity**	**MCC**	**F1-score**	**FNR**	**Specificity**	**Precision**
CRNN [103] [110]	0.850 943	0.171 429	0.828 571	0.029 63	0.8543 48	0.544 647	0.908 671	0.145 652	0.8285 71	0.970 37
RNN [103]	0.769 811	0.214 286	0.785 714	0.040 761	0.7673 91	0.406 494	0.852 657	0.232 609	0.7857 14	0.959 239
CNN [110]	0.766 038	0.228 571	0.771 429	0.043 478	0.7652 17	0.394 398	0.850 242	0.234 783	0.7714 29	0.956 522
FLI- DA- CRNN	0.924 528	0.042 857	0.957 143	0.007 042	0.9195 65	0.747 414	0.954 853	0.080 435	0.9571 43	0.992 958
					Dataset 2					
Techniques	**Accuracy**	**FPR**	**NPV**	**FDR**	**Sensitivity**	**MCC**	**F1-score**	**FNR**	**Specificity**	**Precision**
CRNN [103] [110]	0.876 601	0.124 242	0.875 758	0.319 066	0.8793 97	0.695 776	0.767 544	0.120 603	0.8757 58	0.680 934
RNN [103]	0.754 366	0.262 121	0.737 879	0.517 964	0.8090 45	0.473 339	0.604 128	0.190 955	0.7378 79	0.482 036
CNN [110]	0.763 679	0.230 303	0.769 697	0.506 667	0.7437 19	0.454 361	0.593 186	0.256 281	0.7696 97	0.493 333
FLI- DA- CRNN	0.896 391	0.103 03	0.896 97	0.276 423	0.8944 72	0.738 618	0.8	0.105 528	0.8969 7	0.723 577

Table 4.3: Continued.

Dataset 3										
Techniques	Accuracy	FPR	NPV	FDR	Sensitivity	FNR	MCC	F1-score	Specificity	Precision
CRNN [103] [110]	0.872 902	0.114 846	0.885 154	0.460 674	0.8	0.2	0.586 903	0.644 295	0.8851 54	0.539 326
RNN [103]	0.752 998	0.246 499	0.753 501	0.661 654	0.75	0.25	0.379 163	0.466 321	0.7535 01	0.338 346
CNN [110]	0.736 211	0.268 908	0.731 092	0.676 056	0.7666 67	0.233 333	0.368 654	0.455 446	0.7310 92	0.323 944
FLI- DA- CRNN	0.923 261	0.084 034	0.915 966	0.340 909	0.9666 67	0.033 333	0.759 19	0.783 784	0.9159 66	0.659 091
Dataset 4										
Techniques	Accuracy	FPR	NPV	FDR	Sensitivity	FNR	MCC	F1-score	Specificity	Precision
CRNN [103] [110]	0.887 742	0.119 508	0.880 492	0.266 667	0.9077 67	0.092 233	0.741 117	0.811 28	0.8804 92	0.733 333
RNN [103]	0.725 161	0.279 438	0.720 562	0.511 254	0.7378 64	0.262 136	0.413 162	0.588 008	0.7205 62	0.488 746
CNN [110]	0.732 903	0.279 438	0.720 562	0.501 577	0.7669 9	0.233 01	0.438 075	0.604 207	0.7205 62	0.498 423
FLI- DA- CRNN	0.901 935	0.096 661	0.903 339	0.229 167	0.8980 58	0.101 942	0.765 694	0.829 596	0.9033 39	0.770 833

Table 4.4: Performance analysis of email spam detection using improved deep learning algorithms for cyber security among various machine learning techniques

Dataset 1										
Techniques	**Accuracy**	**FPR**	**NPV**	**FDR**	**Sensitivity**	**FNR**	**MCC**	**F1-score**	**Specificity**	**Precision**
SVM [109]	0.807547	0.214286	0.785714	0.03866	0.81087	0.18913	0.456078	0.879717	0.785714	0.96134
NN [111]	0.818868	0.1	0.9	0.018519	0.806522	0.193478	0.528915	0.885442	0.9	0.981481
KNN [110]	0.818868	0.142857	0.857143	0.026042	0.813043	0.186957	0.507904	0.886256	0.857143	0.973958
DT [108]	0.820755	0.157143	0.842857	0.028424	0.817391	0.182609	0.50363	0.887839	0.842857	0.971576
FLI-DA- CRNN	0.924528	0.042857	0.957143	0.007042	0.919565	0.080435	0.747414	0.954853	0.957143	0.992958
Dataset 2										
Techniques	**Accuracy**	**FPR**	**NPV**	**FDR**	**Sensitivity**	**FNR**	**MCC**	**F1-score**	**Specificity**	**Precision**
NN [111]	0.814901	0.177273	0.822727	0.427007	0.788945	0.211055	0.553686	0.663848	0.822727	0.572993
DT [108]	0.82305	0.180303	0.819697	0.417544	0.834171	0.165829	0.585882	0.68595	0.819697	0.582456
SVM [109]	0.831199	0.175758	0.824242	0.405594	0.854271	0.145729	0.607431	0.701031	0.824242	0.594406
KNN [110]	0.826542	0.180303	0.819697	0.413194	0.849246	0.150754	0.597824	0.694045	0.819697	0.586806
FLI- DA- CRNN	0.896391	0.10303	0.89697	0.276423	0.894472	0.105528	0.738618	0.8	0.89697	0.723577

Table 4.4: Continued.

Techniques	Accuracy	FPR	NPV	Sensitivity	FDR	FNR	MCC	F1-score	Specificity	Precision
Dataset 3										
SVM [109]	0.83693	0.165266	0.834734	0.85	0.536364	0.15	0.545338	0.6	0.834734	0.463636
NN [111]	0.822542	0.182073	0.817927	0.85	0.560345	0.15	0.52315	0.579545	0.817927	0.439655
DT [108]	0.803357	0.196078	0.803922	0.8	0.59322	0.2	0.470559	0.539326	0.803922	0.40678
KNN [110]	0.822542	0.182073	0.817927	0.85	0.560345	0.15	0.52315	0.579545	0.817927	0.439655
FLI- DA- CRNN	0.923261	0.084034	0.915966	0.966667	0.340909	0.033333	0.75919	0.783784	0.915966	0.659091
Dataset 4										
KNN [110]	0.809032	0.188049	0.811951	0.800971	0.393382	0.199029	0.567318	0.690377	0.811951	0.606618
DT [108]	0.830968	0.168717	0.831283	0.830097	0.359551	0.169903	0.614828	0.723044	0.831283	0.640449
NN [111]	0.836129	0.158172	0.841828	0.820388	0.34749	0.179612	0.620176	0.726882	0.841828	0.65251
SVM [109]	0.84	0.173989	0.826011	0.878641	0.353571	0.121359	0.648011	0.744856	0.826011	0.646429
FLI- DA- CRNN	0.901935	0.096661	0.903339	0.898058	0.229167	0.101942	0.765694	0.829596	0.903339	0.770833

Table 4.5: Performance analysis of ensemble approaches

Measures \ Techniques	Voting classifier	LSTM_CNN	Adaboost	Suggested FLI- DA-CRNN
Dataset 1				
FPR	0.14286	0.11429	0.08571	0.04286
Accuracy	0.77170	0.84057	0.77736	0.92453
NPV	0.85714	0.88571	0.91429	0.95714
Specificity	0.85714	0.88571	0.91429	0.95714
FDR	0.02786	0.01914	0.01695	0.00704
FNR	0.24130	0.10870	0.24348	0.08043
MCC	0.44602	0.64441	0.48225	0.74741
F1-score	0.85226	0.93394	0.85504	0.95485
Sensitivity	0.75870	0.89130	0.75652	0.91957
Precision	0.97214	0.98086	0.98305	0.99296
Dataset 2				
FPR	0.04091	0.12576	0.06667	0.10303
Accuracy	0.79627	0.83242	0.79511	0.89639
NPV	0.95909	0.87424	0.93333	0.89697
Specificity	0.95909	0.87424	0.93333	0.89697
FDR	0.34615	0.31439	0.39640	0.27642
FNR	0.74372	0.09045	0.66332	0.10553
MCC	0.31624	0.71670	0.33961	0.73862
F1-score	0.36823	0.78186	0.43226	0.8
Sensitivity	0.25628	0.90955	0.33668	0.89447
Precision	0.65385	0.68561	0.60360	0.72358

Table 4.5: Continued.

Techniques / Measures	Voting classifier	LSTM_CNN	Adaboost	Suggested FLI- DA-CRNN
Dataset 3				
FPR	0.0	0.12325	0.0	0.08403
Accuracy	0.85851	0.82770	0.85851	0.92326
NPV	1.0	0.8767	1.0	0.915
Specificity	1.0	0.87675	1.0	0.91597
FDR	0.0	0.45361	0.0	0.34091
FNR	0.98333	0.11667	0.98333	0.03333
MCC	0.11959	0.63141	0.11959	0.75919
F1-score	0.03279	0.67516	0.03279	0.78378
Sensitivity	0.01667	0.88333	0.01667	0.96667
Precision	1.0	0.54639	1.0	0.65909
Dataset 4				
FPR	0.11775	0.07030	0.05272	0.09666
Accuracy	0.83258	0.76774	0.77806	0.90194
NPV	0.88225	0.92970	0.94728	0.90334
Specificity	0.88225	0.92970	0.94728	0.90334
FDR	0.26908	0.37736	0.31915	0.22917
FNR	0.11650	0.67961	0.68932	0.10194
MCC	0.724405	0.32153	0.34906	0.76570
F1-score	0.8	0.42308	0.42667	0.82960
Sensitivity	0.88350	0.32039	0.31068	0.89806
Precision	0.73092	0.62264	0.68085	0.77083

Table 4.6: Examination of errors in the deployed email spam detection method utilizing a deep learning algorithm to enhance cybersecurity through a comparison of current and proposed studies.

Dataset 1				
Among algorithms				
WOA [106]	DA [102]	PSO [104]	GWO [105]	FLI-DA-CRNN
0.13206	0.10943	0.12830	0.11698	0.075472
Among classifier 1:				
RNN [103]	CNN [110]	CNN-RNN [103] [110]	FLI-DA-CRNN	
0.23019	0.23396	0.14905	0.07547	
Among classifier 2:				
SVM [109]	NN[111]	KNN [110]	DT [108]	FLI-DA-CRNN
0.19245	0.18113	0.18113	0.17925	0.07547
Dataset 2				
Among algorithms				
DA [102]	WOA [106]	GWO [105]	PSO [104]	FLI-DA-CRNN
0.11758	0.11292	0.11991	0.12224	0.10361
Among classifier 1:				
CNN-RNN[103] [110]	RNN [103]	CNN [110]	FLI-DA-CRNN	
0.12340	0.24563	0.23632	0.10361	
Among classifier 2:				
SVM [109]	KNN [110]	NN [111]	DT [108]	FLI-DA-CRNN
0.16880	0.17346	0.18510	0.17695	0.10361
Dataset 3				
Among algorithms				
DA [102]	GWO[105]	PSO [104]	WOA[106]	FLI-DA-CRNN
0.12230	0.10072	0.11511	0.10552	0.07674

Table 4.6: Continued.

Among classifier 1:				
CNN-RNN [103] [110]	RNN [103]	CNN [110]	FLI-DA-CRNN	
0.12710	0.24700	0.26379	0.07674	
Among classifier 2:				
NN [111]	SVM	KNN [110]	DT [108]	FLI-DA-CRNN
0.17746	0.16307	0.17746	0.19664	0.076739
Dataset 4				
Among algorithms				
GWO [105]	WOA[106]	DA [102]	PSO [104]	FLI-DA-CRNN
0.11613	0.12645	0.11742	0.12516	0.09806
Among classifiers 1:				
CNN-RNN [103] [110]	RNN [103]	CNN [110]	FLI-DA-CRNN	
0.11226	0.27484	0.26710	0.09806	
Among classifiers 2:				
SVM [109]	NN [111]	KNN [110]	DT [108]	FLI-DA-CRNN
0.16000	0.16387	0.19097	0.16903	0.09806

4.5 Analysis of Deployed Ensemble Approaches

Table 4.5 illustrates the analysis of four datasets for the overall ensemble methods. The new classifiers are Voting_classifier, LSTM_CNN and Adaboost. The Voting_classifier is employed for classification and detection tasks in the field of machine learning. Detection of fake news is achieved through the application of LSTM_CNN. The Adaboost classifier is employed for enhancing the accuracy of classifiers.

4.6 Error and Feature Analysis of Email Spam Detection Techniques

The error and feature analysis of detection of spam technique is displayed in Table 4.6.

Table 4.7: Implementation time series for algorithm analysis.

Techniques	PSO [104]	GWO [105]	WOA [106]	DA [102]	FLI-DA
Algorithmic time series (seconds)	450	421	398	356	348

Table 4.8: Implementation time series for classifier analysis 1.

Techniques	CNN [110]	RNN [103]	CNN+RNN [103] [110]	FLI-DA- CRNN
Classifier time series (seconds)	450	421	398	348

Table 4.9: Implementation time series for classifier analysis 2.

Techniques	SVM [109]	NN [111]	KNN [110]	DT [108]	FLI-DA-CRNN
Classifier time series (seconds)	186	179	189	192	171

4.7 Analysis of Implementation Time

Tables 4.7, 4.8, and 4.9 present an analysis of time series data for use in classifier and algorithmic analysis in email spam detection via improved deep learning algorithms for cybersecurity purposes. The algorithmic runtimes for WOA, DA, GWO, PSO, and FLI- DA-CRNN are 398, 356, 421, 450, and 348 seconds, respectively. The classification time for RNN as well as CNN is 421 and 450 seconds in classifier analysis 1. The classifier time for both RNN and CNN was 398 seconds. The classifier time for FLI-DA-CRNN was 348 seconds. The time series for KNN, DT, NN, SVM, and FLI-DA-CRNN in classifier analysis 2 were 189,192, 179, 186, and 171.

4.8 Conclusion

TF-IDF is used to determine the count of spam words, which were initially extracted from the textual features. The GLCM and color correlogram were selected as the visual features, whereas FLI-DA was utilized for the enhancement of hidden neurons in RNNs and CNNs, as well as for optimal feature selection. The neurons embedded within both RNN and CNN architectures were improved through the use of FLI-DA. Both CNNs and RNNs were used to categorize the data into spam and ham. The FLI-DA-CRNN model demonstrated superior accuracy, outperforming SVM by 10.32%, KNN by 12.24%, NN by 12.24%, and DT by 14.93%. In comparison with deep learning methods, machine learning methodologies and optimization techniques, the FLI-DA-CRNN achieved the most effective outcome in identifying spam. As a result, the improved model for email spam detection yielded effective outcomes. Therefore, the enhanced model of e-mail spam detection gave effectual results.

CHAPTER

5

Email Spam Detection Approach II: Adaptive Capsule Network Based – An Automated Email Spam Detection Approach

5.1 Introduction

This chapter throws light on Adaptive Capsule Network based – An Automated Email Spam Detection Approach for email spam detection. Emails often contain malicious viruses and spyware that are classified as spam. Recognizing junk emails is crucial due to their adaptable nature. Several methods involving machine learning and optimization algorithms are explored to detect phishing emails, focusing on accurately distinguishing junk emails while minimizing the volume of spam messages. Problems associated with numerous spam emails that pose a threat to computer systems are resolved by employing this approach. Conventional models for detecting spam emails are not effective in identifying spam emails using both image and text data. This study proposes an innovative and sophisticated framework for identifying spam emails through the use of both text and image data, incorporating advanced deep learning methods. The key components of this spam email detection model are the design of an A-CapsNet and the implementation of multi-objective feature selection (MOFS).

Two methods, including TF-IDF and TV, are used for extracting features from text data. Three methods, FDA, WHT, and color correlograms, are implemented for extracting features from image data. A hybrid optimization method known as the G-SFO algorithm has been developed to address MOFS, as it seems the features' length is considerable and requires reduction to mitigate the challenges encountered during training. An advanced framework called

DOI: 10.1201/9788743810384-5

A-CapsNet is also employed for detecting spam emails, building on the progress made by the proposed G-SFO algorithm. To effectively illustrate the precise identification of spam emails as achieved by the proposed model, it is compared to numerous established methods and computer algorithms.

5.2 Architecture Of The Proposed Email Spam Detection Technique using the G-SFO Algorithm

Email is a crucial component in facilitating both economic and ongoing business communications. The escalating popularity of email services has led to a corresponding surge in unwanted emails. Research is currently focused on resolving the problems associated with detecting spam emails. Existing email spam detection models that utilize machine learning techniques face challenges in assessing emails containing only embedded text, as well as those featuring visual elements such as texture, color, and shape in images. This lays the groundwork for developing a deep-learning framework to identify spam email. The suggested deep-learning framework for detecting email spam is illustrated in Figure 5.1.

Figure 5.1: A framework for detecting spam emails using deep learning techniques.

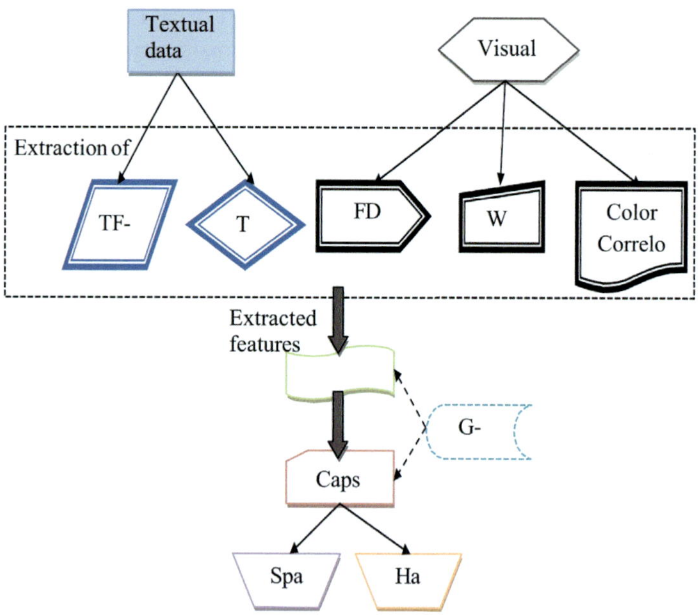

The proposed framework seeks to develop an automatic MOFS technique for a deep learning- based framework designed to detect spam emails. This framework for detecting spam emails utilizes the image and textual datasets to perform feature extraction. Extracting the characteristics from the visual and textual data is crucial for obtaining the relevant features and eliminating the irrelevant ones. Techniques like the color correlogram, WHT, and FDA are employed to extract features from visual information, whereas methods such as TV and TF-IDF are utilized to extract features from textual data. The suggested G-SFO algorithm optimally selects these features, with the goal of reducing the feature's length. The G-SFO algorithm for carrying out MOFS is achieved by combining the GWO and SFO algorithms as a source of inspiration.

The A-CapsNet framework is specifically designed to identify spam emails through the application of the G-SFO algorithm, which is used to tackle the complexities of a multi-objective function. The parameters of the A-CapsNet, including the quantity of hidden neurons, are adjusted by the proposed G-SFO algorithm. The A-CapsNet architecture classified emails into either legitimate or spam categories. This framework's efficiency in spam email detection is achieved by integrating a novel MOFS method and leveraging the A-CapsNet architecture, which is founded on the proposed G-SFO algorithm. This methodology prioritizes both the precision and the accuracy of the categorized outcome.

5.3 Extraction of Visual Features

The data in the dataset is used to obtain the input for extracting the features. In this model, multiple techniques are employed to extract features from both visual and textual data. This process involves reducing the number of dimensions in the input data provided. The goal is to identify the most fundamental and complete set of characteristics from the provided data set. As a result, this enhances data processing speed and decreases the amount of storage needed.

Visual features are extracted from image data using WHT, FDA, and color correlogram methods.

5.3.1 Walsh–Hadamard transform matrix

Among the various methods developed for visual transformation, the WHT [112] is one example. Due to its characteristics, including a faster computing process, robustness, straightforward construction and operation, flexibility, and minimal energy consumption, this method appears to be an optimal selection for extracting features from the image dataset. The goal is to distinguish between attributes such as texture and edge characteristics. The fundamental components of the WHT yield orthogonal results, resulting in binary values of either −1 or +1. The WHT's operation is simplified by its use of standard subtraction and addition as the fundamental process. The WHTM is expressed by the form presented in Eq. 5.1.

$$j_{gg} = \begin{bmatrix} j_{gg-1} & j_{gg-1} \\ j_{gg-1} & -j_{gg-1} \end{bmatrix} \tag{5.1}$$

The values of the second- and fourth-order WHTM are given by Eq. (5.1) and Eq. (5.2).

$$j_2 = \begin{bmatrix} 1 & 1 \\ 1 & -1 \end{bmatrix} \tag{5.2}$$

$$j_4 = \begin{bmatrix} 1 & 1 & 1 & 1 \\ 1 & 1 & -1 & -1 \\ 1 & -1 & -1 & 1 \\ 1 & -1 & 1 & -1 \end{bmatrix} \tag{5.3}$$

The basic vectors in the WHTM are orthogonal and orthonormal. The transform of the WHT j(i,0) is given by Eq. (5.4).

$$j(i,o) = \sum_{cc=1}^{ff} \sum_{ee=1}^{ff} px(cc,ee) * p(cc,ee,l,o) \tag{5.4}$$

The term $px(cc, ee)$ in Eq. (5.4) denotes the pixel of the image data, ff denotes the image size, and $p(cc, ee,l, o)$ denotes the function of the kernel.

5.3.2 Fisher discriminate analysis

The commonly employed approach for reducing the image's dimensionality is FDA [113]. The scatter matrix for each sub-class is calculated according to Eq. 5.5.

$$q_{hh} = \sum_{r \in \bar{s}} \left(s_{hh} - s_{\bar{hh}}\right) \left(s_{hh} - s_{\bar{hh}}\right)^{u} \tag{5.5}$$

The term shh in Eq. (5.5) denotes the sample data matrix, s_{hh} denotes the mean of the sample matrix, and q denotes the scatter matrix of the hhth sub-class. The scatter matrix of the entire sub- class is denoted by Eq. (5.6).

$$q_t = \sum_{hh=1}^{ij} s_{hh} \tag{5.6}$$

In Eq. (5.6), the term *jj* denotes the total count of the classes. The scatter matrix of the between classes is computed using Eq. (5.7).

$$q_{ii} = \sum_{r \in \bar{s}} v_{hh} \left(s_{\bar{hh}} - \bar{s} \right) \left(s_{\bar{hh}} - \bar{s} \right)^{u} \tag{5.7}$$

The term v_{hh} hh in Eq. (5.7), represents the overall number of observations within a *hh* class. Components of the FDA are derived only when the ratio of the between-class scatter matrix to the within-class scatter matrix reaches its maximum value. This condition is illustrated in Eq. (5.8).

$$w(t) = \frac{t^{u} q_{ii} t}{t^{u} q_{t} t} \tag{5.8}$$

In Eq. (5.8), the term *t* denotes the optimum direction of the Fisher discriminant. The Eigen vectors for the problems regarding Eigen values are estimated using Eq. (5.9).

$$q_{ii} t = \gamma q_{t} t \tag{5.9}$$

The term γ in Eq. (5.9) denotes the range of separability among the classes. The conventional problem of Eigen values is estimated using Eq. (5.10), provided that the matrix *qt* is non-singular.

$$q_{t}^{-1} q_{ii} t = \gamma q_{t} t \tag{5.10}$$

The total count of the FDA components represents the total count of the classes. There is a total of *jj*–1 Eigen values of non-zero values.

5.3.3 Color correlogram

The color correlogram [114] technique involves using the histograms of colors as feature vectors to extract image features. The color histogram method's effectiveness in extracting image data features stems from its insensitivity to minute variations and the absence of complex computations in the screening positions. Implementing the system is challenging due to its susceptibility to false positives and decreased resilience when faced with larger datasets. The development of the color correlogram is aimed at resolving these issues. The statement clarifies the regional spatial correlation of the worldwide distribution of color. This method effectively extracts the visual features from both ham and spam images. In Chapter 3, a detailed explanation of the color correlogram is provided. The image features extracted using the WHT, FDA, and color correlogram methods are represented as *OF im* . Approximately 771 features are extracted from the image data. From the obtained visual featuresOF_{lf}^{img}, the G-SFO selects VF_{kl}^{feat}as optimal image features.

5.4 Extraction of Text Features

5.4.1 TV

Features from textual data are extracted using a combination of TV and TF-IDF methods.

The TV method assigns a relevance score to each attribute based on how far it varies from its mean value. This score is a measure of how much each attribute contributes to the overall characteristics of the document. The traits that are not evenly distributed across the entire document are extracted by the TV method. It is also more eloquent than the evenly distributed characteristics because it highlights the unique features that set the document apart. The features obtained by TV are mathematically formulated as Eq. (5.11).

$$x_{kk} = \frac{1}{y}\sum_{ll=1}^{y}\left(z_{kkll} - \bar{z_{kk}}\right)_2 \tag{5.11}$$

In Eq. (5.11), the term y denotes the entire count of the document in the text.

5.4.2 TF-IDF

A digital statistical method called TF-IDF [116] is used to determine the frequency of spam words in a text collection. In text mining and information modeling, TF-IDF serves as a weighting element. For a detailed description of TF-IDF refer Chapter 3. The textual features obtained fromThe textual features obtained from the TV and TF-IDF techniques are denoted by a OF_{gx}^{txt} notation. The total number of extracted features from the image data falls in a range of 600. From the obtained textual features, G-SFO selects TF^{feat} the optimal text features.

5.5 Architecture of the A-CapsNet Framework for Email Spam Detection

The email is categorized as either spam or legitimate using the A-CapsNet framework with the G-SFO algorithm. The G-SFO algorithm's optimally selected attributes are fed into the A- CapsNet for enhanced classification performance. The G-SFO algorithm optimizes the number of hidden units in the CapsNet architecture.

CapsNet [117] is used due to its rapid learning capacity to effectively manage data transitions and its capacity to perform rotations to enhance detection precision. One of CapsNet's key advantages is its routing by agreement functionality. The outcome of the higher-level capsule is expected to precede those of the lower-level capsules. CapsNet is effective for feature extraction, data classification, and pose parameter collection, specifically for learning good weights. The network consists of a multitude of neurons that collaborate to represent diverse parameter poses based on their respective activity vectors. The remaining possibility of the spatial features is signified by the length of this vector. The CapsNet architecture involves the use of multiple layers to facilitate the routing by agreement process.

Results from the first layer are then propagated upwards to the parent capsules in the subsequent layer, considering the agreed-upon routing process. The capsule's coefficient of coupling does not have an equivalent value. All the remaining capsules are trying to recognize the output from the parent capsule. Confirmation of the detection parent capsule's actual outcomes enhances the coefficient of coupling between the two capsules. The detection of the aa^{th} capsule's result for the parent capsule $a^{'}$ is calculated using Eq. (5.12).

$$a^{'}_{bb|aa} = b_{aabb} a_{aa} \tag{5.12}$$

In Eq. (5.12), the term a denotes the output of the aath capsule and b denotes the aa $aabb$ weighted matrix of coefficients. The degree of confirmation among the parent and capsule of the lower level is formed by the coefficient of coupling, which is obtained using Eq. (5.13).

$$d_{aabb} = \frac{\exp\left(c_{aabb}\right)}{\sum_{dd} \exp\left(c_{aadd}\right)} \tag{5.13}$$

The term c_{aabb} in Eq. (5.13) denotes the log function that represents the possibility in which the aath capsule is related to the bbth capsule. The value of c is taken as zero initially. The parent capsule's input ebb is given by Eq. (5.14).

$$e_{bb} = \sum_{aa} d_{aabb}\, a^{'}_{bb|aa} \tag{5.14}$$

The output from the entire capsule at the final stage f_{bb} is evaluated using Eq. (5.15).

$$f_{bb} = \frac{\|e_{bb}\|^2 e_{bb}}{1 + \|e_{bb}\|^2 \|e_{bb}\|} \tag{5.15}$$

The agreement is used to upgrade the coefficient of coupling with the possibility of the log h_{aabb} that is determined using Eq. (5.16).

$$h_{aabb} = f_{bb} \cdot a'_{bb|aa} \tag{5.16}$$

The loss function at the final layer of every capsule is determined using Eq. (5.17).

$$g_{dd} = m_{dd} \cdot \max\left(0, n^+ - \|f_{dd}\|\right)^2 + \varphi\left(1 - m_{dd}\right) \cdot \left(0, \|f_{dd}\| - n^-\right)^2 \tag{5.17}$$

The emails are finally categorized as either ham or spam with the assistance of the G-SFO algorithm. The A-CapsNet framework for detecting spam email is illustrated in Figure 5.2.

The primary objective of integrating the G-SFO algorithm within the developed A- CapsNet framework for spam email filtering is to attain enhanced

Figure 5.2: Structure of the designed A-CapsNet framework for spam email detection.

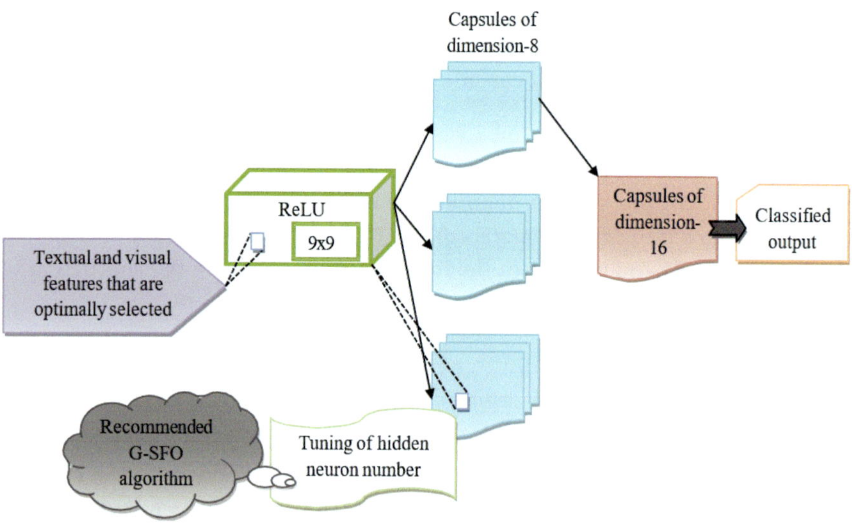

precision and accuracy in categorizing spam versus non-spam emails. The A-CapsNet structure is adjusted by optimizing the number of hidden neurons, with the assistance of the G-SFO algorithm, and the most relevant features are selected from the textual and image data. This objective is represented by Eq. (5.18).

$$cc = \arg\min_{\{TF_{ih}^{\text{feat}}, VF_{kl}^{\text{feat}}, hr_{op}^{ACN}\}} \left(\frac{1}{af + pf}\right) \tag{5.18}$$

In Eq. (5.18), the term *pf* represents the maximized precision, *af* represents maximized accuracy, TF_{ih}^{feat} represents the tuned textual features, VF_{kl}^{feat} denotes the tuned visual features, and hr_{op}^{ACN} represents the tuned number of hidden neurons. The precision is computed by using Eq. (5.19).

$$pf = \frac{tp}{tp + fp} \tag{5.19}$$

In Eq. (5.19), the true positives are denoted by the term *tp* and the false positive is denoted by the term *fp*. The accuracy is determined using Eq. (5.20).

$$af = \frac{tp + nt}{tp + fp + nt + nf} \tag{5.20}$$

In Eq. (5.20), the term *nt* represents the true negatives and *nf* denotes the false negatives. The results of this model's classification are very precise and accurate.

5.6 G-SFO – Gray-sail Fish Optimization Algorithm

5.6.1 MOFS – multi-objective feature selection by G-SFO

Feature selection is employed to identify the most crucial relevant inputs, thereby reducing the number of inputs and making further analysis and processing simpler. The most relevant characteristics need to be extracted for further analysis due to the abundance of visual and textual features. In this work, the G-SFO algorithm recently implemented performs the MOFS process. The process of MOFS is illustrated in Figure 5.3.

Figure 5.3: Process of MOFS by the implemented G-SFO algorithm.

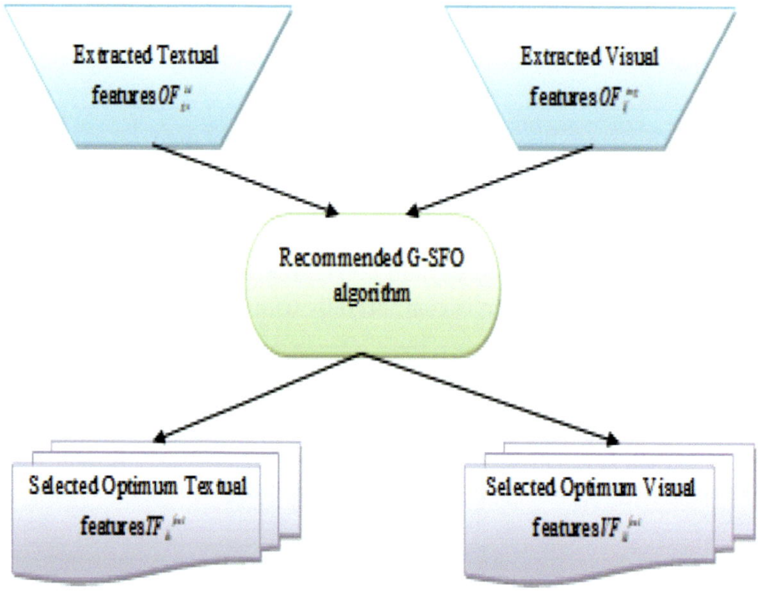

5.6.2 Gray-sailfish optimization (G-SFO) tuning

The primary motivation behind the SFO [118] algorithm, a population-based optimization algorithm, stems from the differing hunting methods employed by groups of sailfish when hunting their prey collectively. The SFO demonstrates the fastest rate of convergence for multimodal problems, and it is also a highly effective optimizer for non-separable functions. The SFO algorithm is used to obtain prominent outputs for non-separable, scalable, and non-convex test functions. Due to its non-complicated design, the GWO [119] is very simple to implement. It requires significantly less storage space and converges at a faster rate. The novel G-SFO algorithm has been implemented for the proposed model to facilitate the effective classification of spam emails and also MOFS. The detection of spam emails occurs more quickly with the aid of the most effective features that have been obtained.

To enhance the accuracy of the classified results, CapsNet optimizes the number of hidden neurons it employs. The GWO and SFO algorithm characteristics are integrated to formulate the G-SFO algorithm. The SFO algorithm offers several advantages, as it achieves good performance in both low-dimensional and high-dimensional spaces, and yields outcomes that outcompete those of other algorithms. It effectively mitigates the issue of getting stuck in suboptimal local minima, achieves a more harmonious balance between exploitation and exploration, accelerates convergence rates, and enhances overall efficiency. In contrast, the SFO method involves a more intricate computational procedure. The GWO algorithm [120] is paired with the SFO algorithm to accelerate the process of finding the optimal solution. The GWO algorithm is simpler to implement due to its reduced reliance on governing parameters and excels at resolving diverse heuristic-based problems. The power of attack A servers is the foundation for the G-SFO algorithm that has been implemented.

The solution is upgraded by the SFO algorithm when $A < 1/2$ when the attack power reaches a certain threshold $A < 1/2$, a random variable is then checked. If the arbitrary variable's value equals $B < 1/2$, the GWO algorithm uses the alpha's location to improve the solution, otherwise if $B < 1/2$, the beta's location is used to improve the solution. The following section introduces the sailfish optimization algorithm and the Grey Wolf Otimizer.

5.6.3 Sail fish optimization

SFO [118]: The variation in the hunting behavior adopted by the group of sailfish while hunting prey in a group is the primary source of motivation for the SFO algorithm. The sailfish attempts to catch its target, which consists of sardines. Not the entire school of sardines is destroyed; only a small number are killed, and the rest are left severely harmed. The sailfish's altered hunting behavior drives the SFO algorithm's motivation.

The sailfish's availability location is specified in Eq. 5.21.

$$C_D = \begin{bmatrix} C_{1,1} & C_{1,2} & \cdots & C_{1,F} \\ C_{2,1} & C_{21,2} & \cdots & C_{2,F} \\ \vdots & \vdots & \ddots & \vdots \\ C_{oo,1} & C_{oo,2} & \cdots & C_{oo,F} \end{bmatrix} \tag{5.21}$$

In Eq. (5.21), the term *F* represents the dimension, *CD* represents the location matrix, *Cmm,nn* represents the present location of the sailfish which is given by $C_{mm,nm} \in (mm = 1, 2, 3, \ldots, oo)$, and *oo* represents the total count of the sailfish in the group. The fitness function for the sailfish *Gsf* is given by Eq. (5.22).

$$G(sf) = G(C_1, C_2, \ldots, C_{oo}) \tag{5.22}$$

The fitness function for the entire clan of sailfish is given by Eq. (5.23).

$$G_{sf} = \begin{bmatrix} G\left(C_{1,1}, C_{1,2}, \ldots, C_{1,F}\right) \\ G\left(C_{2,1}, C_{2,2}, \ldots, C_{2,F}\right) \\ \vdots \\ G\left(C_{oo,1}, C_{oo,2}, \ldots, C_{oo,F}\right) \end{bmatrix} = \begin{bmatrix} G_{C_1} \\ G_{C_2} \\ \vdots \\ G_{C_{oo}} \end{bmatrix} \tag{5.23}$$

The location of the prey is computed using Eq. (5.24).

$$H_D = \begin{bmatrix} H_{1,1} & H_{1,2} & \cdots & H_{1,F} \\ H_{2,1} & H_{2,2} & \cdots & H_{2,F} \\ \vdots & \vdots & \ddots & \vdots \\ H_{pp,1} & H_{pp,2} & \cdots & H_{pp,F} \end{bmatrix} \tag{5.24}$$

The fitness value of the prey is shown by Eq. (5.25).

$$H_{sa} = \begin{bmatrix} G\left(H_{1,1}, H_{1,2}, \ldots, H_{1,F}\right) \\ G\left(H_{2,1}, H_{2,2}, \ldots, H_{2,F}\right) \\ \vdots \\ G\left(H_{pp,1}, H_{pp,2}, \ldots, H_{pp,F}\right) \end{bmatrix} = \begin{bmatrix} G_{H_1} \\ G_{H_2} \\ \vdots \\ G_{H_{oo}} \end{bmatrix} \tag{5.25}$$

The key reason for deriving the solution from the SFO algorithm is the combination of prey and sailfish. In the lookup area, the sailfish captures its prey and, as a result, upgrades its position within the searching stage. The elite position in the ideal location is therefore shown by J_C^{mm}. The optimal prey item, which has the highest fitness value, is selected for capture and is referred to as J_H^{mm}. At every cycle, the sailfish's position is updated. The updated position of the sailfish at a particular iteration *mm* is described by Eq. (5.26).

$$newJ_C^{mm} = J_C^{mm} - \eta \times \left(B(0,1) \times \left(\frac{J_C^{mm} + J_H^{mm}}{2} \right) - \text{old}\,{}_C^{mm} \right) \tag{5.26}$$

In Eq. (5.26), the term B represents the arbitrary variable and η denotes a coefficient. The value of B is in the range $[0, 1]$. The coefficient η is found using Eq. (5.27).

$$\eta_{mm} = 2 \times B(0,1) \times K - K \tag{5.27}$$

The term *K* in Eq. (5.27), denotes the volume of the school of prey. This can be evaluated using Eq. (5.28).

$$K = 1 - \left(\frac{M_C}{M_C + M_H} \right) \tag{5.28}$$

In Eq. (5.28), the terms M_H and M_C denote the number of prey in the school, and the number of sailfish, respectively. The value of $M_C = M_H \times N$ denotes the population of the prey that contributes to the population of the sailfish. The new ideal prey is computed using Eq. (5.29).

$$newJ_H^{mm} = L \times (J_C^{mm} - oldJ_C^{mm} + A) \tag{5.29}$$

In Eq. (5.29), the term A represents the attack power of the sailfish and L denotes an arbitrary variable of range [0,1]. The value of the attack power A is given by Eq. (5.30).

$$A = \Re \times (1 - (2 \times P \times \kappa)) \tag{5.30}$$

The term k denotes a coefficient that linearly reduces the value of the attack power A from $\Re \to 0$. The population of the prey λ depending on the attack power of the sailfish, and its corresponding coefficient k is formulated with the help of Eq. (5.31) and Eq. (5.32).

$$\lambda = M_H \times A \tag{5.31}$$

$$\kappa = qq_{mm} \times A \tag{5.32}$$

$$A = \Re \times (1 - (2 \times P \times \kappa)) \tag{5.33}$$

In Eq. (5.33), the term J_H^{mm} denotes the present location of the prey and J_C^{mm} represents the present location of the sailfish. The upgrade of the solution is done by the SFO algorithm when $A < 1/2$, or else, the GWO algorithm is used to upgrade the solution.

5.7 Grey wolf optimization

The grey wolf pack's hunting behavior is the basis for the GWO algorithm as mentioned in GWO [119]. Let the first, second, and third optimal solutions be represented by ν, μ, and ρ respectively. The remaining options are referred to as τ. The hunting is conducted by ν, μ, and ρ wolves, with the remaining wolves following these dominant individuals. The three main stages of the GWO algorithm comprise hunting, targeting, and fighting. In the implemented GSFO algorithm, if the attack power exceeds a certain level $A \geq \frac{1}{2}$, then the arbitrary variable is checked. If the value of the arbitrary variable is $B < 1/2$, then the alpha's location in the GWO algorithm is used to upgrade the solution, or else, if $B \geq \frac{1}{2}$, then the location of the beta is used to upgrade the solution. The location of the alpha and beta wolves is provided by Eq. (5.34) and Eq. (5.35).

$$\vec{Q}(v) = \vec{Q}_v - \vec{R}_1 \cdot \left(\vec{S}_v\right) \tag{5.34}$$

$$\vec{Q}(\mu) = \vec{Q}_\mu - \vec{R}_2 \cdot \left(\vec{S}_\mu\right) \tag{5.35}$$

The coefficient vector $\vec{R}$ is computed using Eq. (5.36).

$$\vec{R} = 2\vec{U} \cdot \overrightarrow{V1} - \vec{U} \tag{5.36}$$

The term $\overrightarrow{V1}$ in Eq. (4.36) denotes an arbitrary variable in the range $[0, 1]$ and $\vec{U}$ denotes an element that reduces linearly from $2 \rightarrow 0$. The coefficient

Algorithm 5.1: Recommended G-SFO algorithm				
The population of the prey school and the sailfish are initialized				
The parameters of the algorithms are initialized				
The fitness of the prey and the sailfish are computed				
The ideal sailfish and the ideal prey are evaluated				
	While (till termination)			
		For every sailfish		
			Using Eq. (4.27), evaluate the value of η	
			The location of the sailfish is upgraded Eq. (4.26)	
		End		
		The attack power A is determined using Eq. (4.30)		
		If $A < \frac{1}{2}$		
			The value of λ and k are determined using Eq. (4.31) and Eq (4.32)	
			With the help of λ and k select the school of prey	
			The location of the prey is used to upgrade the solution with the implementation of Eq. (4.29)	
		Else		
			If $B > \frac{1}{2}$	
				The GWO algorithm is used to upgrade the solution
				The location of the alpha wolf is used to upgrade the solution
			Else	
				The location of the beta wolf is used to upgrade the solution
			End	
		End		
		The fitness value of the prey is determined		
		If the ideal solution is available in the prey		
		The hunted prey is replaced by the sailfish using Eq. (4.33)		
		The injured prey is removed		
		The ideal prey and the sailfish are upgraded		
		End		
	End			
Return				

matrix $\vec{W}$ is computed using Eq. (5.37).

$$\vec{W} = a \cdot \vec{V2} \tag{5.37}$$

The term $\vec{V2}$ in Eq. (5.37), represents an arbitrary variable in the range $[0, 1]$. The location of the alpha and beta wolves is shown by Eq. (5.38).

$$\vec{S_v} = \left| \vec{W_1} \cdot \vec{Q_v} - \vec{Q} \right| ; \vec{S_\mu} = \left| \vec{W_2} \cdot \vec{Q_\mu} - \vec{Q} \right| \tag{5.38}$$

Consequently, the G-SFO algorithm developed aims to enhance the convergence characteristics of the proposed spam email detection model (Figure 5.4). For effective classification, the hybrid algorithm speeds up the computational

Figure 5.4: Flowchart of the proposed G-SFO algorithm.

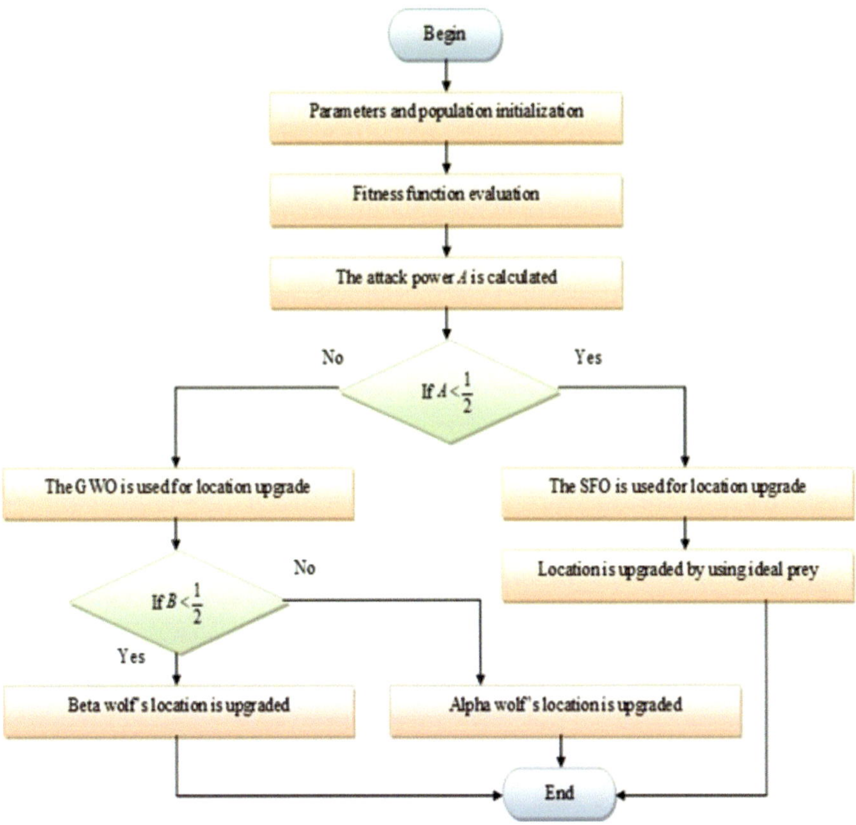

process and accelerates the rate at which convergence occurs. The recommended G-SFO algorithm employs multi-objective functions to select the optimal features. The G-SFO algorithm begins by initializing the population. The fitness function is then set up. The arbitrary variables and attack power are then evaluated. The GWO and SFO methods are utilized to update the solutions. The best fitness function is then utilized to update the solutions, thereby facilitating the selection of the most suitable ones for the proposed model. The G-SFO algorithm's execution process is detailed in Algorithm 5.1.

CHAPTER

6

Performance Analysis of G-SFO with AcapsNetwork

6.1 Experimental Setup and Parameter Settings

The specified spam email detection framework was implemented using Python, and an examination was conducted to demonstrate its effectiveness. The performance of the proposed model for email spam detection was evaluated by comparing it with existing models in terms of FNR, NPV, MCC, accuracy, sensitivity, F1-score, FPR, FDR, specificity, and precision. The experiment was carried out using a test group of 10 individuals and was limited to a maximum of 25 rounds of iterations. The G-SFO-CapsNet framework for identifying spam email was compared to established algorithms such as WOA-CapsNet [121], PSO-CapsNet [122], SFO-CapsNet [118], and GWO-CapsNet [119], as well as conventional classifiers including KNN [123], DT [124], NN [125], SVM [126], RNN [127], CapsNet [128], and CNN [129].

6.2 Dataset Used

The recommended spam email detection framework was developed using four datasets: the Spam mails dataset, the Ling-spam dataset, the Image spam dataset, and the Spam-or-ham email classification dataset. A detailed account of the collected data is presented in Chapter 3.

DOI: 10.1201/9788743810384-6

6.3 Evaluation Metrics

The results of the proposed model for identifying spam emails are compared with other classifiers and algorithms using specific validation metrics listed below, which include:

(A) Determination of the NPV *nv* as described in Eq. (6.1).

$$nv = \frac{nt}{nt + nf} \tag{6.1}$$

(B) The F1-score *fc* is computed with the help of Eq. (6.2).

$$f_c = \frac{tp}{2tp + fp + nf} \tag{6.2}$$

(C) The FDR *dr* is evaluated using Eq. (6.3).

$$dr = \frac{fp}{tp + fp} \tag{6.3}$$

(D) The MCC *mw* is determined with the help of Eq. (6.4).

$$mw = \frac{(tp \times nt) - (fp \times nf)}{\sqrt{(tp + fp)(tp + nf)(tn + nf)(tn + fp)}} \tag{6.4}$$

(E) The specificity *sfp* is evaluated using Eq. (6.5).

$$sfp = \frac{nt}{fp + nt} \tag{6.5}$$

(F) The FNR *fn* is computed using the formula provided in Eq. (6.6).

$$fn = \frac{nf}{tp + tn} \tag{6.6}$$

(G) The sensitivity is evaluated with the help of Eq. (6.7).

$$sni = \frac{tp}{tp + nf} \tag{6.7}$$

(H) The FPR is calculated using Eq. (6.8).

$$fr = \frac{fp}{fp + tn} \tag{6.8}$$

6.4 Algorithmic Evaluation of the Suggested G-SFO with the ACapsNet Model

The algorithmic evaluation of the proposed email spam detection model using Datasets 1, 2, 3, and 4 is illustrated in Figures 6.1, 6.2, 6.3, and 6.4. The evaluation process is performed by adjusting the model's learning percentage. Figure 6.1 (a) shows that the false positive rate (FPR) of the proposed G-SFO-CapsNet model for email spam detection is 4.55% lower than the WOA-CapsNet and PSO-CapsNet models and 5.13% lower than the SFO-CapsNet and GWO-CapsNet models at a learning rate of 65%. Comparing data in Figure 6.1 (b), it is evident that the FNR of the G-SFO-CapsNet model for detecting email spam is 50%, 13.79%, 28.57%, and 53.36% lower than that of the WOA-CapsNet, GWO-CapsNet, PSO-CapsNet, and SFO-CapsNet models, respectively, when trained at a learning rate of 35%. The results from Figure 6.1 (c) indicate that the proposed G-SFO-CapsNet model outperforms the WOA-CapsNet, PSO-CapsNet, SFO- CapsNet, and GWO-CapsNet models by 1.5%, 1.03%, 0.7%, and 1.3%, respectively, when the learning percentage is 65%. According to Figure 6.1 (d), the F1-score of the proposed G-SFO- CapsNet model outperforms the SFO-CapsNet, GWO-CapsNet, WOA-CapsNet, and PSO- CapsNet models by 1.05%, 0.38%, 0.72%, and 0.44%, respectively when trained at a 35% learning rate. Figure 4.5 (e) reveals that the G-SFO-CapsNet model for email spam detection exhibits improved precision, being 0.48% and 0.69% more accurate than SFO-CapsNet and GWO-CapsNet, and 0.25% more precise than WOA-CapsNet and PSO-CapsNet at a 35% learning rate.

6.5 Performance Analysis of the G-SFO Acapsnet Model with Machine and Deep Learning Models

The performance of the email spam detection framework against traditional classifiers is demonstrated in Figures 6.5, 6.6, 6.7, and 6.8 for Datasets 1, 2, 3, and 4, respectively. The model's performance is assessed by adjusting its learning rate. According to Figure 6.5 (a), the F1-score of the proposed G-SFO-CapsNet framework for email spam detection is 0.15% higher than CapsNet, RNN, CNN, NN, and SVM, and 0.05% and 0.03% more than existing KNN and DT, respectively, when the learning percentage is set at 35%. The G-SFO-CapsNet framework for email spam detection achieved accuracy of 2.3%, 1.1%, 4.7%, 3.5%, 4.7%, 3.5%, and 3.5% greater than KNN, DT, NN, SVM, RNN, CNN, and CapsNet, respectively, at an overall accuracy of 55%, as indicated in Figure 6.5 (b).

Figure 6.1: Dataset 1 based algorithmic evaluation of the suggested email spam detection model in terms of (a) FPR, (b) FNR, (c) accuracy, (d) F1-score, and (e) precision.

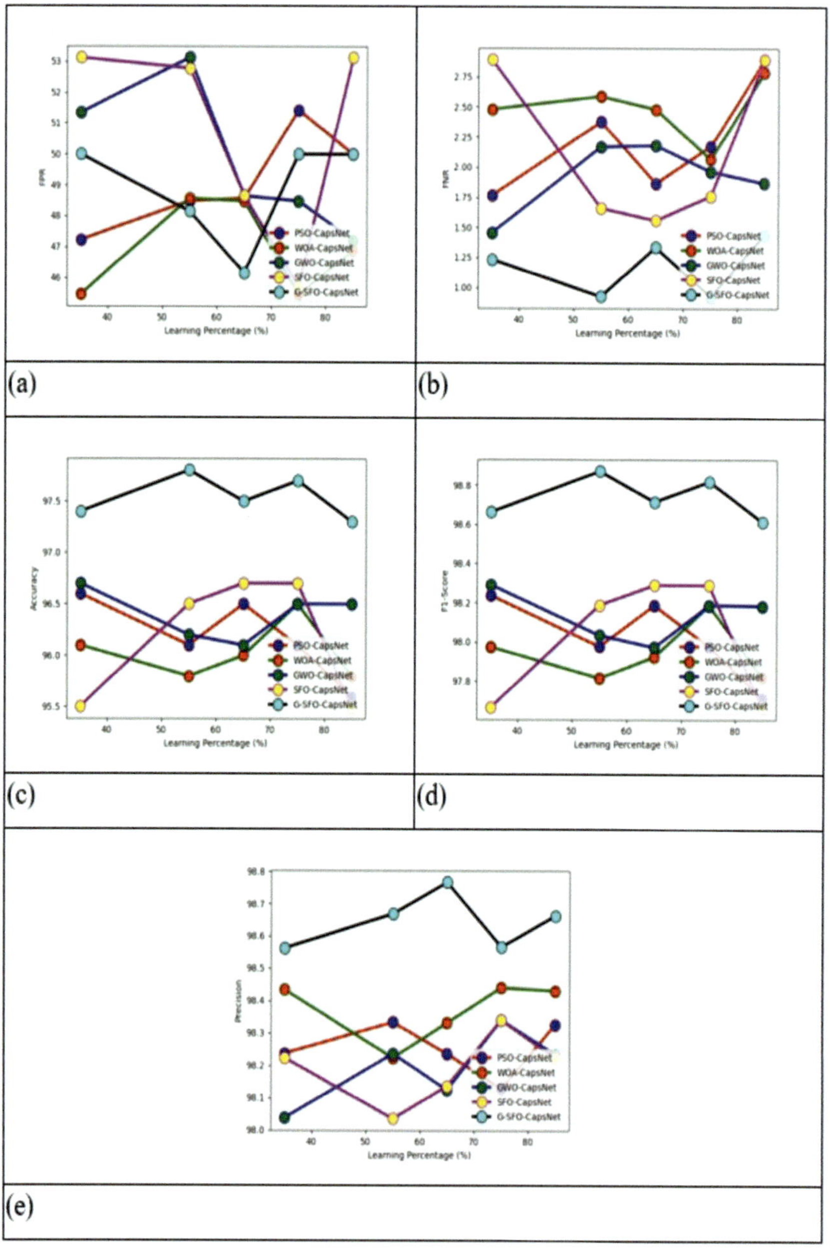

Figure 6.2: Dataset 2 based algorithmic evaluation of the implemented email spam detection model in terms of (a) FPR, (b) FNR, (c) accuracy, (d) F1-score, and (e) precision.

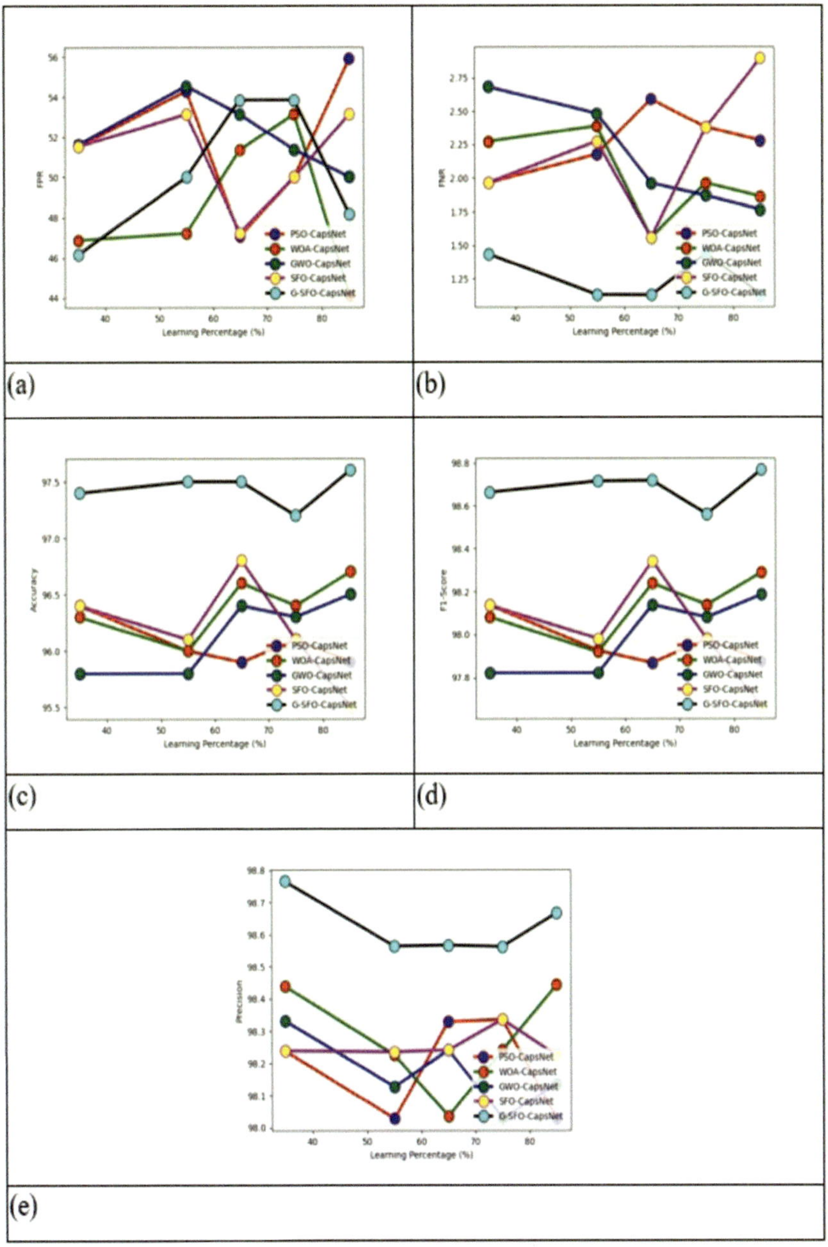

Figure 6.3: Dataset 3 based algorithmic evaluation of the recommended email spam detection model in terms of (a) FPR, (b) FNR, (c) accuracy, (d) F1-score, and (e) precision.

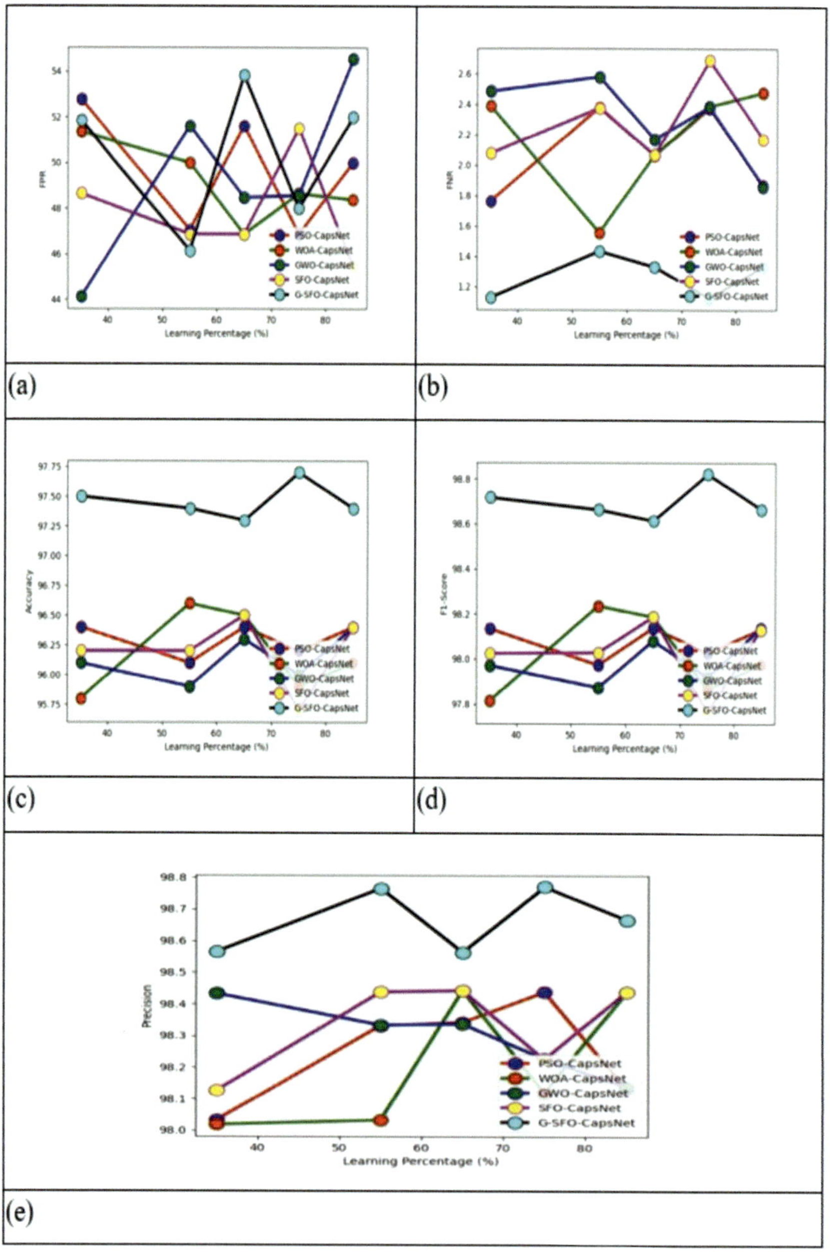

Figure 6.4: Dataset 4 based algorithmic evaluation of the designed email spam detection model in terms of (a) FPR, (b) FNR, (c) accuracy, (d) F1-score, and (e) precision.

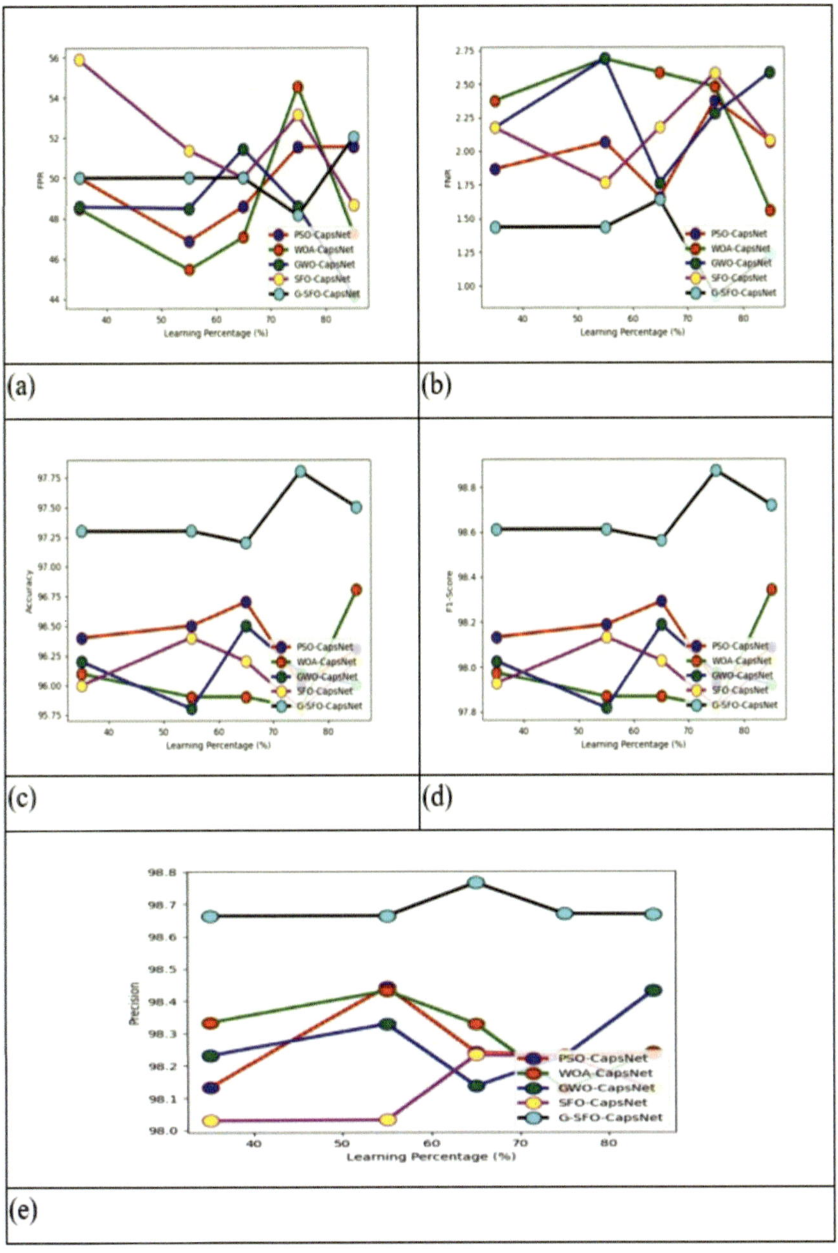

Figure 6.5: Dataset 1 based classifier comparison of the suggested email spam detection framework with respect to (a) F1-score, (b) accuracy, (c) FPR, (d) precision, and (e) FNR

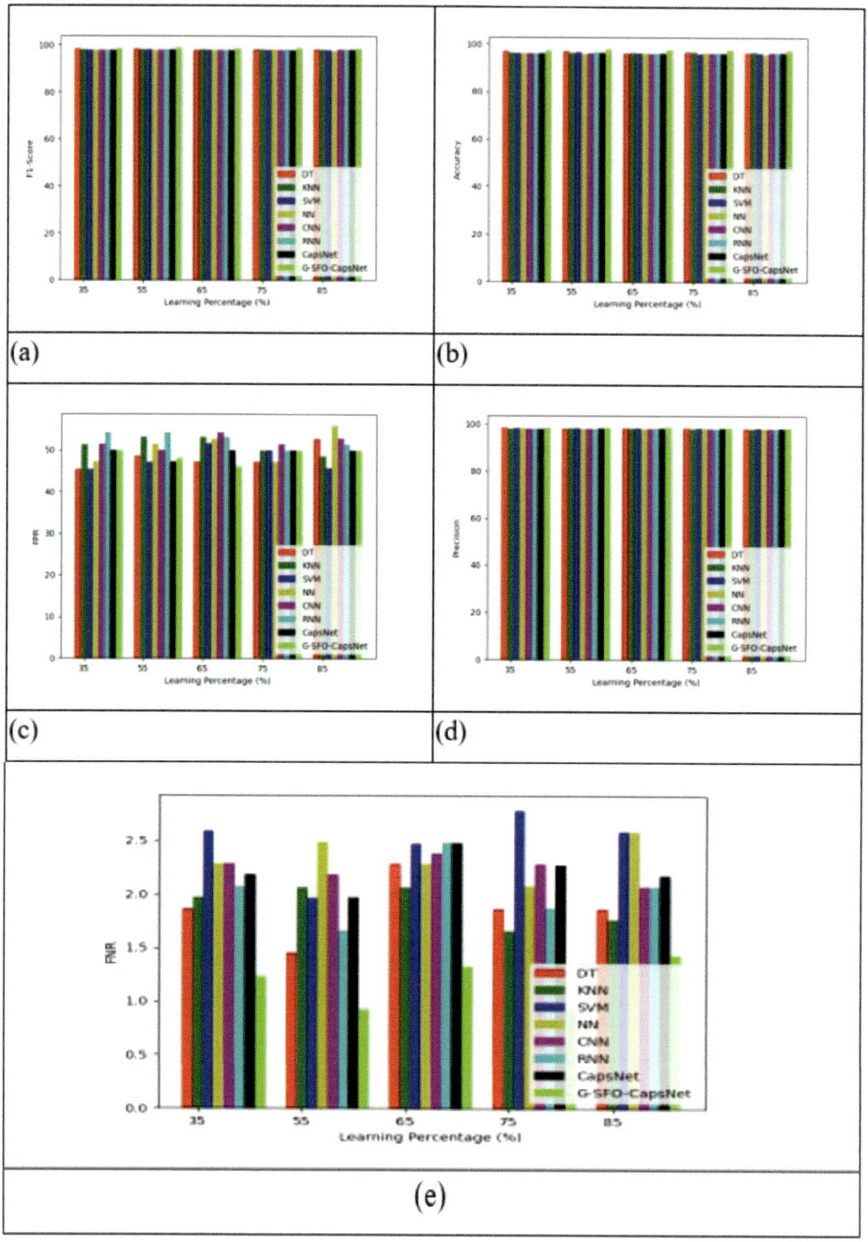

Figure 6.6: Dataset 2 based classifier comparison of the implemented email spam detection framework with respect to (a) F1-score, (b) accuracy, (c) FPR, (d) precision, and (e) FNR.

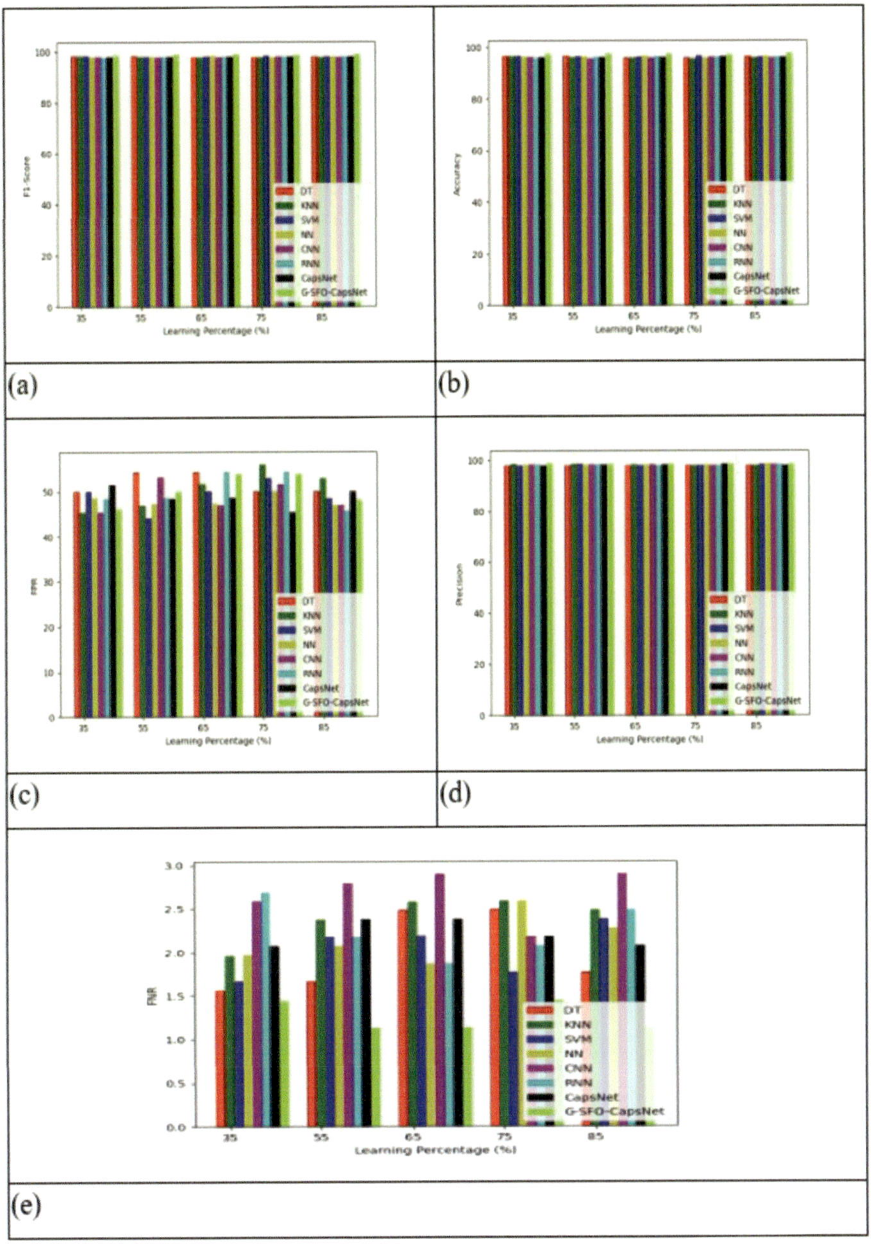

Figure 6.7: Dataset 3 based classifier comparison of the recommended email spam detection framework with respect to (a) F1-score, (b) accuracy, (c) FPR, (d) precision, and (e) FNR.

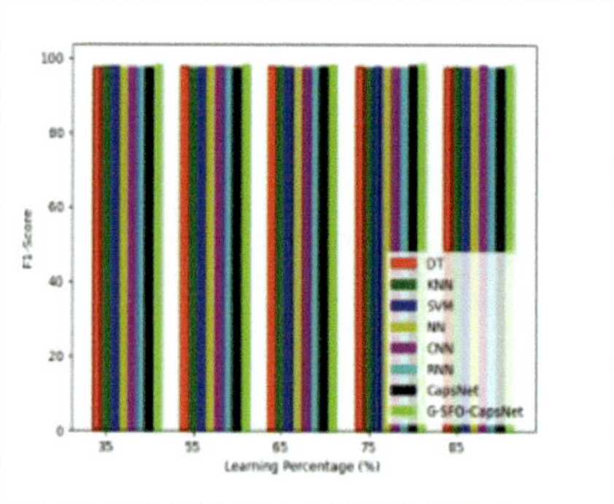

(a)

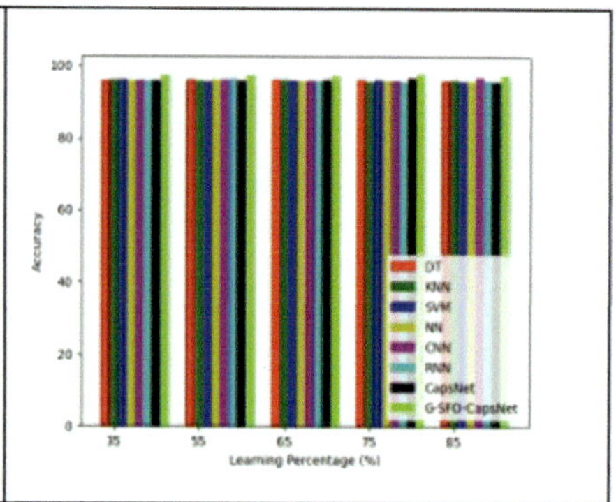

(b)

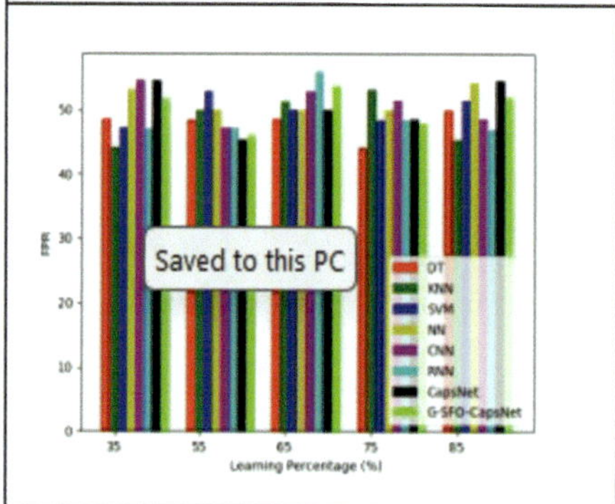

(c)

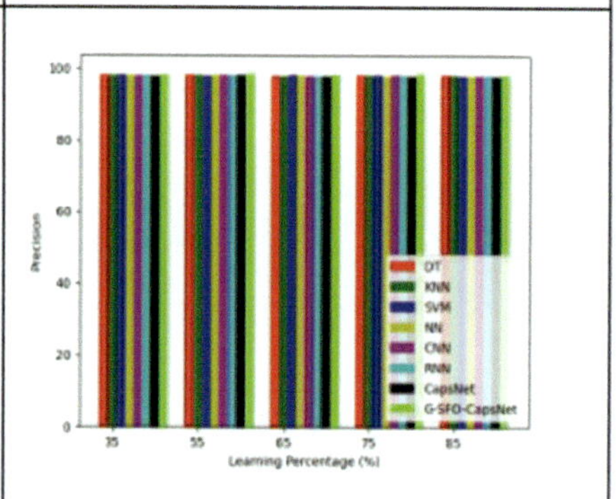

(d)

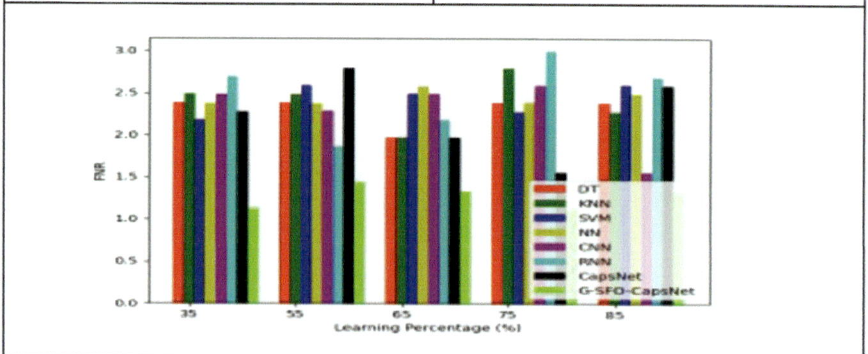

(e)

Figure 6.8: Dataset 4 based classifier comparison of the designed email spam detection framework with respect to (a) F1-score, (b) accuracy, (c) FPR, (d) precision, and (e) FNR.

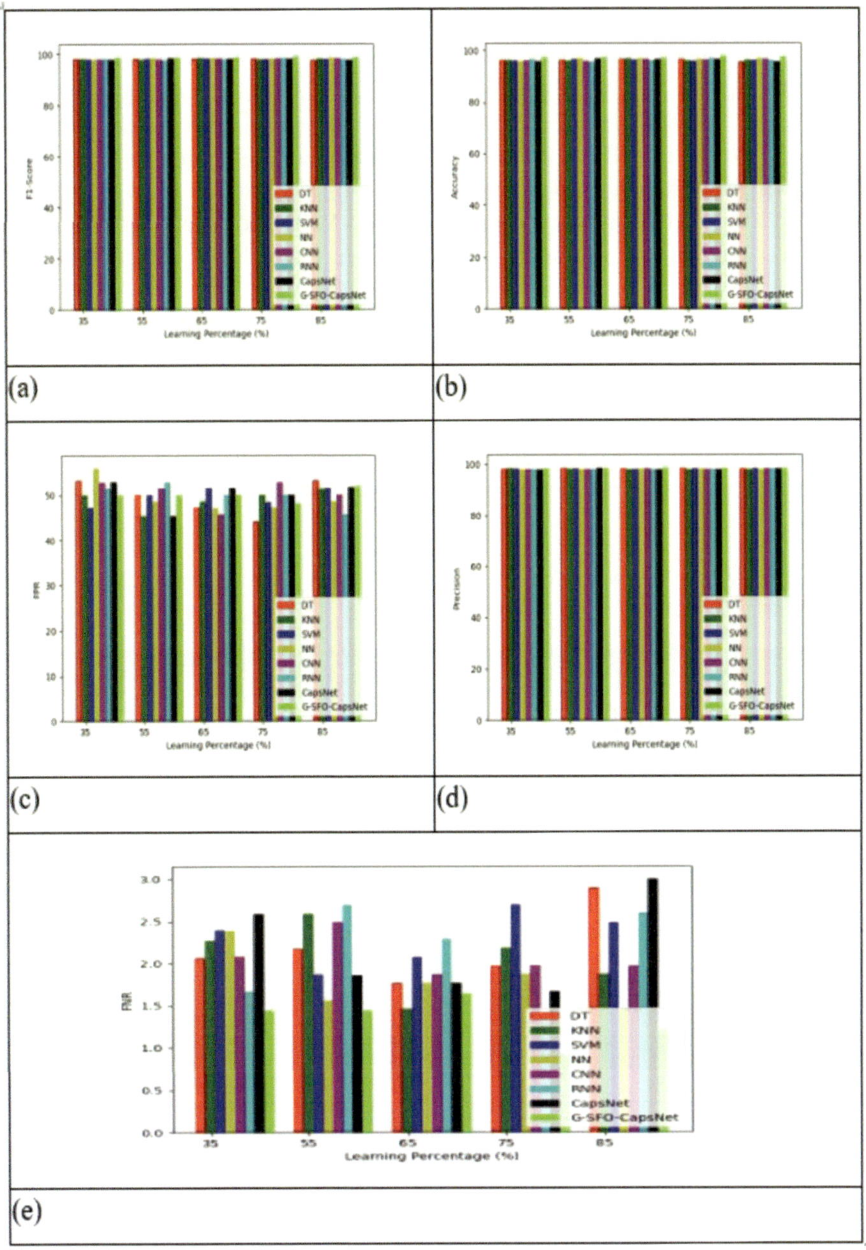

The FPR of the G-SFO-CapsNet framework for email spam detection is seen to be 12.09%, 12.7%, 13.04%, 12.52%, 12.35%, 12.96%, and 4.35% lower than the existing CapsNet, RNN, CNN, NN, SVM, KNN, and DT, respectively, when the learning rate is set at 65%. The results in Figure 6.5 (d) indicate that the G-SFO-CapsNet framework for email spam detection outperformed the conventional KNN, CNN, SVM, DT, NN, CapsNet, and RNN, achieving a precision increase of 2.06%, 4.2%, 1.02%, 1.02%, 3.125%, 3.125%, and 4.2%, respectively, at a 35% learning rate. The FNR of the designed G-SFO-CapsNet framework for email spam detection is found to be 35.14%, 38.46%, 45.45%, 46.67%, 41.46%, 46.67%, and 54.72% lower than the conventional DT, KNN, CapsNet, CNN, RNN, NN, and SVM, respectively, when using a 35% learning rate, as shown in Figure 6.5 (e).

6.6 Performance Analysis of the G-SFO ACapsNet Model with Existing MetaHeuristic Algorithms

The performance of the developed spam email detection model in relation to Datasets 1, 2, 3, and 4 is illustrated in Table 6.1, where it is compared to existing

Table 6.1: Performance evaluation of the suggested email spam detection framework with conventional algorithms.

Measures	WOA-CapsNet [121]	SFO-CapsNet [118]	PSO-CapsNet [122]	GWO-CapsNet [119]	G-SFO-CapsNet
Dataset 1					
Precision	0.984	0.982	0.983	0.982	0.987
FPR	0.469	0.531	0.500	0.472	0.500
Sensitivity	0.972	0.971	0.971	0.981	0.986
F1-score	0.978	0.977	0.977	0.982	0.986
FDR	0.016	0.018	0.017	0.018	0.013
MCC	0.432	0.382	0.404	0.502	0.477
FNR	0.028	0.029	0.029	0.019	0.014
NPV	0.531	0.469	0.500	0.528	0.500
Accuracy	0.958	0.955	0.956	0.965	0.973
Specificity	0.531	0.469	0.500	0.528	0.500
Dataset 2					
NPV	0.559	0.469	0.441	0.500	0.519
Accuracy	0.967	0.955	0.959	0.965	0.976
F1-score	0.983	0.977	0.979	0.982	0.988
Specificity	0.559	0.469	0.441	0.500	0.519

Table 6.1: Continued.

Measures	WOA-CapsNet [121]	SFO-CapsNet [118]	PSO-CapsNet [122]	GWO-CapsNet [119]	G-SFO-CapsNet
FNR	0.019	0.029	0.023	0.018	0.011
FPR	0.441	0.531	0.559	0.500	0.481
Sensitivity	0.981	0.971	0.977	0.982	0.989
FDR	0.016	0.018	0.020	0.019	0.013
Precision	0.984	0.982	0.980	0.981	0.987
MCC	0.519	0.382	0.402	0.489	0.527
Dataset 3					
MCC	0.435	0.483	0.481	0.436	0.467
Accuracy	0.961	0.964	0.964	0.964	0.974
FDR	0.016	0.016	0.019	0.019	0.013
Specificity	0.516	0.545	0.500	0.455	0.480
FNR	0.025	0.022	0.019	0.019	0.013
FPR	0.484	0.455	0.500	0.545	0.520
Precision	0.984	0.984	0.981	0.981	0.987
NPV	0.516	0.545	0.500	0.455	0.480
F1-score	0.980	0.981	0.981	0.981	0.987
Sensitivity	0.975	0.978	0.981	0.981	0.987
Dataset 4					
FPR	0.472	0.486	0.515	0.441	0.520
FDR	0.018	0.019	0.018	0.016	0.013
Sensitivity	0.984	0.979	0.979	0.974	0.988
F1-score	0.983	0.980	0.981	0.979	0.987
Precision	0.982	0.981	0.982	0.984	0.987
Accuracy	0.968	0.962	0.963	0.960	0.975
MCC	0.527	0.480	0.445	0.471	0.477
NPV	0.528	0.514	0.485	0.559	0.480
Specificity	0.528	0.514	0.485	0.559	0.480
FNR	0.016	0.021	0.021	0.026	0.012

classical heuristic algorithms. The comparison of the email spam detection model, which is based on a dataset of 4, reveals that the proposed G-SFO-CapsNet framework is more accurate than the WOA-CapsNet, SFO-CapsNet, PSO-CapsNet, and GWO-CapsNet models by 0.72%, 1.35%, 1.25%, and 1.56%, respectively. The suggested email spam detection model demonstrates 0.30%, 0.51%, 0.71%, and 0.61% greater precision in its results compared to the WOA-CapsNet, SFO-CapsNet, PSO-CapsNet, and GWO-CapsNet, respectively. It is clear that the proposed G-SFO-CapsNet approach for spam email identification yields more precise and accurate classification outcomes in comparison to other existing methods.

6.7 Performance Validation of the Proposed Spam Email Detection Framework Against Traditional Classifiers

The performance of the proposed spam email detection framework in relation to Datasets 1, 2, 3, and 4 is presented in comparison with traditional classifiers in Table 6.2. The Dataset 3 based validation of traditional classifiers using the recommended email spam detection model reveals that the G-SFO-CapsNet framework achieves accuracy that is 1.14%, 1.78%, 1.56%, 1.46%, 1.78%, 1.78%, and 0.72% higher than the KNN, NN, RNN, DT, CapsNet, SVM, and CNN models, respectively. Using the suggested email spam detection model based on

Table 6.2: Performance examination of the recommended email spam detection model with distinct classifiers.

Validation metrics/ classifier	KNN [123]	NN [125]	RNN [127]	DT [124]	CapsNe [128]	SVM [126]	CNN [128]	G-SFO-CapsNet
Dataset 1								
Precision	0.981	0.980	0.981	0.980	0.982	0.983	0.981	0.987
F1-score	0.982	0.977	0.980	0.981	0.980	0.979	0.980	0.986
FDR	0.019	0.020	0.019	0.020	0.018	0.017	0.019	0.013
Specificity	0.514	0.441	0.486	0.472	0.500	0.543	0.471	0.550
FNR	0.018	0.026	0.021	0.019	0.022	0.026	0.021	0.014
FPR	0.486	0.559	0.514	0.528	0.500	0.457	0.529	0.500
Accuracy	0.965	0.956	0.962	0.963	0.962	0.959	0.962	0.973
NPV	0.514	0.441	0.486	0.472	0.500	0.543	0.471	0.500
MCC	0.502	0.384	0.453	0.460	0.453	0.463	0.438	0.477
Sensitivity	0.982	0.974	0.979	0.981	0.978	0.974	0.979	0.986
Dataset 2								
FPR	0.529	0.469	0.457	0.500	0.500	0.485	0.469	0.481
NPV	0.471	0.531	0.543	0.500	0.500	0.515	0.531	0.519
FDR	0.019	0.016	0.017	0.020	0.019	0.017	0.016	0.013
Specificity	0.471	0.531	0.543	0.500	0.500	0.515	0.531	0.519
MCC	0.412	0.462	0.469	0.495	0.467	0.448	0.426	0.527
Sensitivity	0.975	0.977	0.975	0.982	0.979	0.976	0.971	0.989
FNR	0.025	0.023	0.025	0.018	0.021	0.024	0.029	0.011
Precision	0.981	0.984	0.983	0.980	0.981	0.983	0.984	0.987
F1-score	0.978	0.981	0.979	0.981	0.980	0.980	0.978	0.988
Accuracy	0.958	0.963	0.960	0.964	0.962	0.961	0.957	0.976

Table 6.2: Continued.

Validation metrics/ classifier	KNN [123]	NN [125]	RNN [127]	DT [124]	CapsNe [128]	SVM [126]	CNN [128]	G-SFO-CapsNet
Dataset 3								
FPR	0.455	0.543	0.469	0.500	0.545	0.514	0.486	0.520
MCC	0.476	0.405	0.438	0.440	0.391	0.421	0.519	0.467
FDR	0.016	0.020	0.016	0.018	0.019	0.019	0.019	0.013
Specificity	0.545	0.457	0.531	0.500	0.455	0.486	0.514	0.480
Precision	0.984	0.980	0.984	0.982	0.981	0.981	0.981	0.987
F1-score	0.981	0.978	0.979	0.979	0.978	0.978	0.983	0.987
FNR	0.023	0.025	0.027	0.024	0.026	0.026	0.016	0.013
NPV	0.545	0.457	0.531	0.500	0.455	0.486	0.514	0.480
Accuracy	0.963	0.957	0.959	0.960	0.957	0.957	0.967	0.974
Sensitivity	0.977	0.975	0.973	0.976	0.974	0.974	0.984	0.987
Dataset 4								
FNR	0.019	0.015	0.026	0.029	0.030	0.025	0.020	0.012
Precision	0.980	0.981	0.983	0.982	0.983	0.982	0.983	0.987
FDR	0.020	0.019	0.017	0.018	0.017	0.018	0.017	0.013
Specificity	0.486	0.514	0.543	0.469	0.484	0.485	0.500	0.580
Sensitivity	0.981	0.985	0.974	0.971	0.970	0.975	0.980	0.988
FPR	0.514	0.486	0.457	0.531	0.516	0.515	0.500	0.520
Accuracy	0.963	0.968	0.959	0.955	0.955	0.959	0.965	0.975
NPV	0.486	0.514	0.543	0.469	0.484	0.485	0.500	0.480
MCC	0.474	0.527	0.463	0.382	0.384	0.419	0.460	0.477
F1-score	0.981	0.983	0.979	0.977	0.977	0.979	0.982	0.987

Dataset 2, validation of the traditional classifiers yields more precise results, with improvements of 0.61%, 0.30%, 0.41%, 0.71%, 0.61%, 0.41%, and 0.30% over KNN, NN, RNN, DT, CapsNet, SVM, and CNN, respectively. It is clear that the proposed G-SFO-CapsNet model outperforms other conventional classifiers in terms of achieving more precise and accurate spam email classification outcomes.

6.8 Summary

A novel hybrid meta-heuristic algorithm-based MOFS has been designed in conjunction with A-CapsNet for identifying spam emails. The collected image and text data were pre-processed using a variety of distinct techniques. The G-SFO algorithm was then utilized to select the optimal features. The optimized features were input into the A-CapsNet architecture to produce the classified outcomes. The G-SFO approach was employed to resolve the multi-objective function by optimizing detection accuracy and precision to their maximum levels. The simulation results showed that the suggested model incorporating G-SFO-CapsNet outperformed KNN, NN, RNN, DT, CapsNet, SVM, and CNN by 1.14%, 1.78%, 1.56%, 1.46%, 1.78%, 1.78%, and 0.72%, respectively, in terms of accuracy for Dataset 3.

The precision of the suggested G-SFO-CapsNet email spam detection model was 0.61%, 0.30%, 0.41%, 0.71%, 0.61%, 0.41%, and 0.30% higher than the respective precision of the KNN, NN, RNN, DT, CapsNet, SVM, and CNN models, respectively. The designed spam email detection framework has shown superior performance compared to other algorithms on all four datasets, resulting in enhanced operation and classification accuracy. CapsNet failed to extract the necessary features. The presence of this difficulty resulted in a decline in the overall performance of the proposed spam email detection framework. The future resolution of this issue can be achieved through the implementation of advanced classifier or ensemble methodologies.

CHAPTER

7

Comparative Analysis

7.1 Introduction

In every research paper, a comparative analysis is a major element for analyzing the differences and similarities between the proposed approaches and understanding the identified problem very effectively. Two different email spam identification approaches for providing cybersecurity are considered for the comparative analysis. It makes a good decision about the key issues aroused in the email spam detection approaches. The weakness of the methods is also determined by using this comparative analysis. In the first contribution, the FLI-DA-CRNN model is used for detecting email spam from the collected data. In the second contribution, the G-SFO- capsnet model is suggested to detect email spam from the given dataset. The performance of the two different implemented email spam detection models is formulated in graphical form, and several positive measures and also negative measures are considered for the evaluation. The positive measures like F1-score, precision, accuracy, NPV, sensitivity, specificity and MCC are taken for the performance computation. Moreover, negative measures like FPR, FNR, and FDR are also taken for the computation of performance of the two different email spam detection models.

7.2 Results and Discussions

In the results and discussion section, the performance comparison of two different email spam detection models is carried out via three different datasets. The learning percentage attribute is used for differentiating the performance

DOI: 10.1201/9788743810384-7

between two different email spam detection models. This learning percentage is used to provide resultant outcomes over the extensive data, and it provides accurate results over the detection of email spam.

7.2.1 Comparative analysis of Dataset 1

Figure 7.1 gives the comparative analysis of two different spam detection models for considering Dataset 1. From the analysis, the second contribution performed very well on the negative measure analysis and also the positive measures provide better outcome than the first contribution. In addition, the G-SFO-capsnet-based email spam identification approach attained with enhanced accuracy, sensitivity, specificity and precision of 11.62%, 12.64%, 67.30%, and 1.03% than the FLI-DA-CRNN for learning percentage 35.

Figure 7.1: Continued.

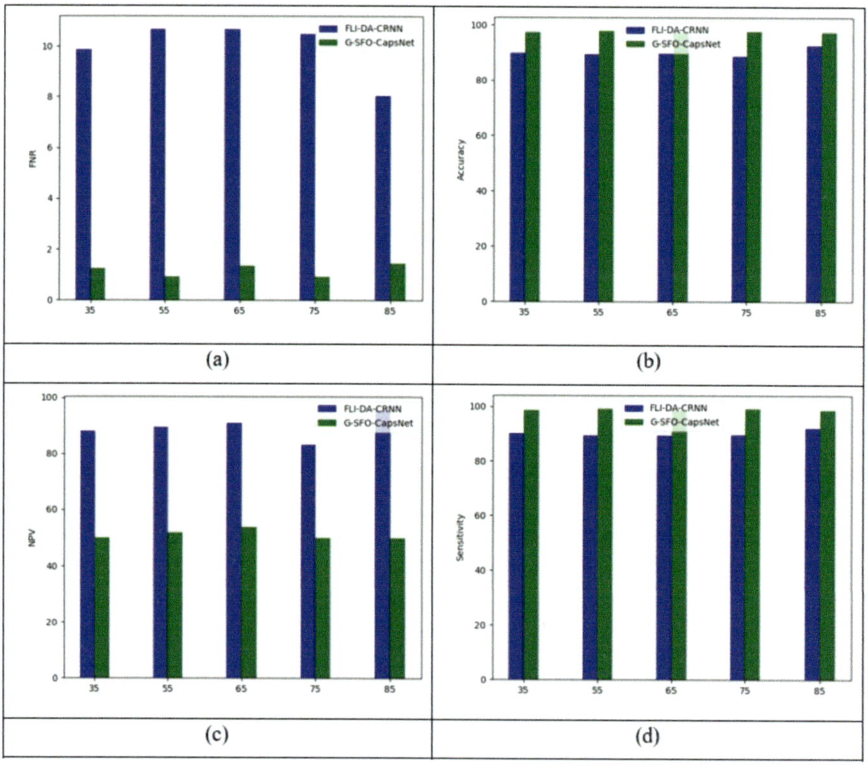

Figure 7.1: Performance computation among two different email spam detection approaches for Dataset 1 in regards to (a) FNR, (b) accuracy, (c) NPV, (d) sensitivity, (e) FDR, (f) Specificity, (g) F1-score, (h) precision, (i) MCC, and (j) FPR.

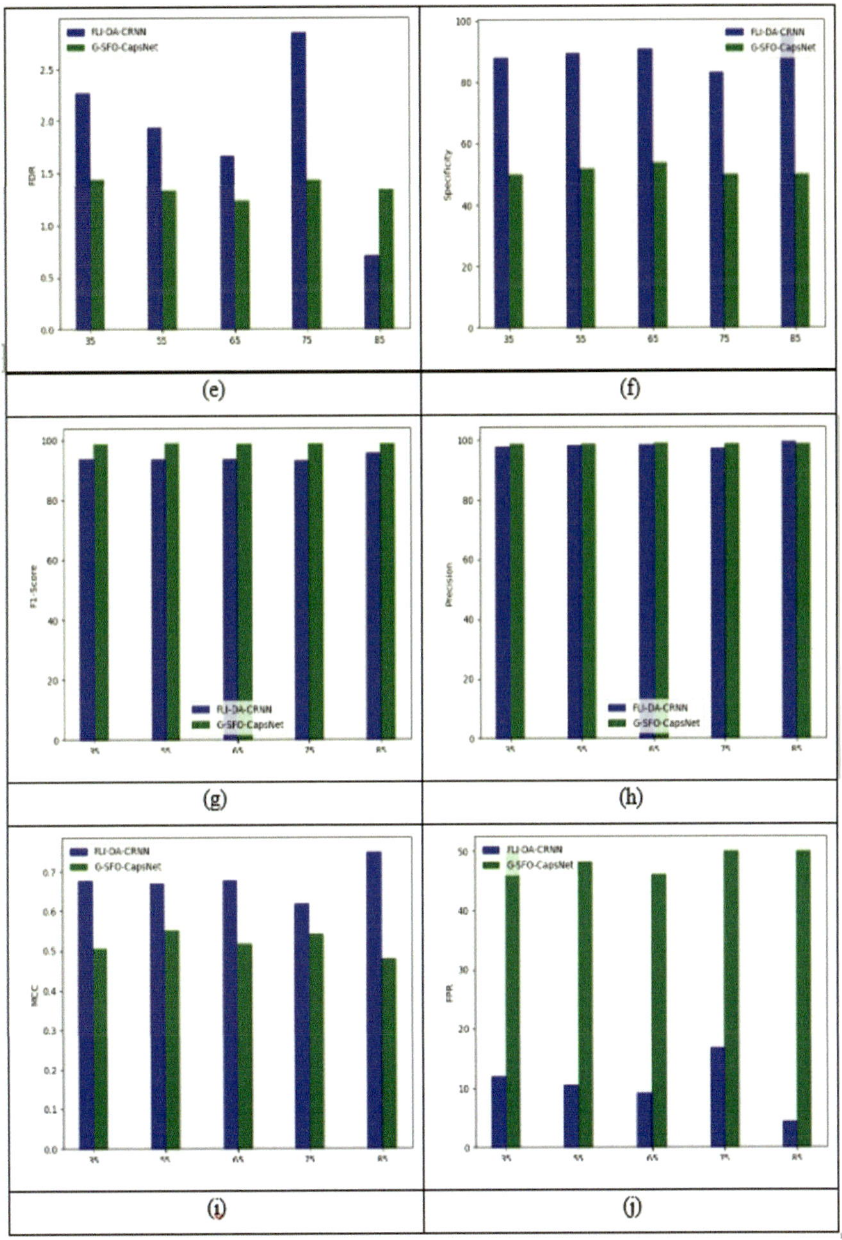

Figure 7.2: Continued.

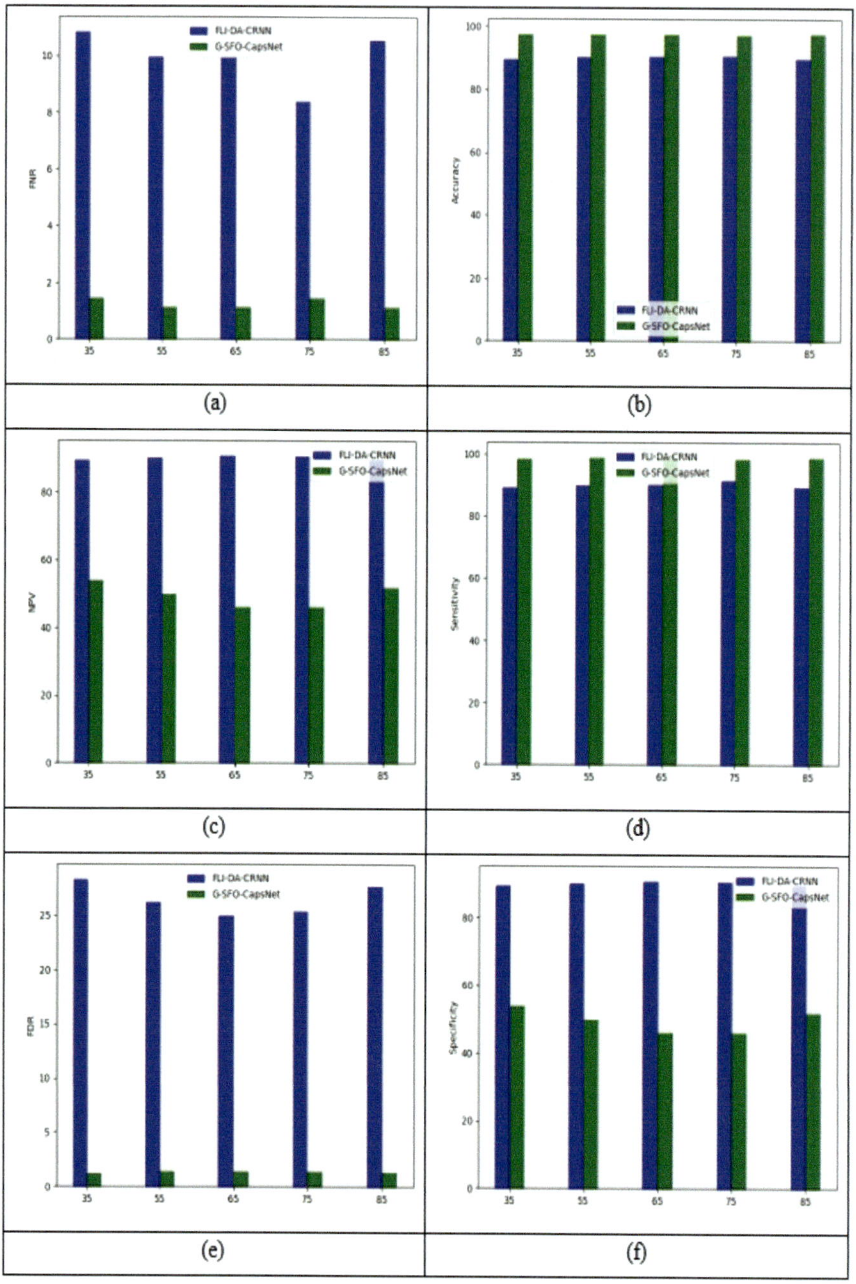

Figure 7.2: Performance computation among two different email spam detection approaches for Dataset 2 in regards to (a) FNR, (b) accuracy, (c) NPV, (d) sensitivity, (e) FDR, (f) specificity, (g) F1-score, (h) precision, (i) MCC, and (j) FPR.

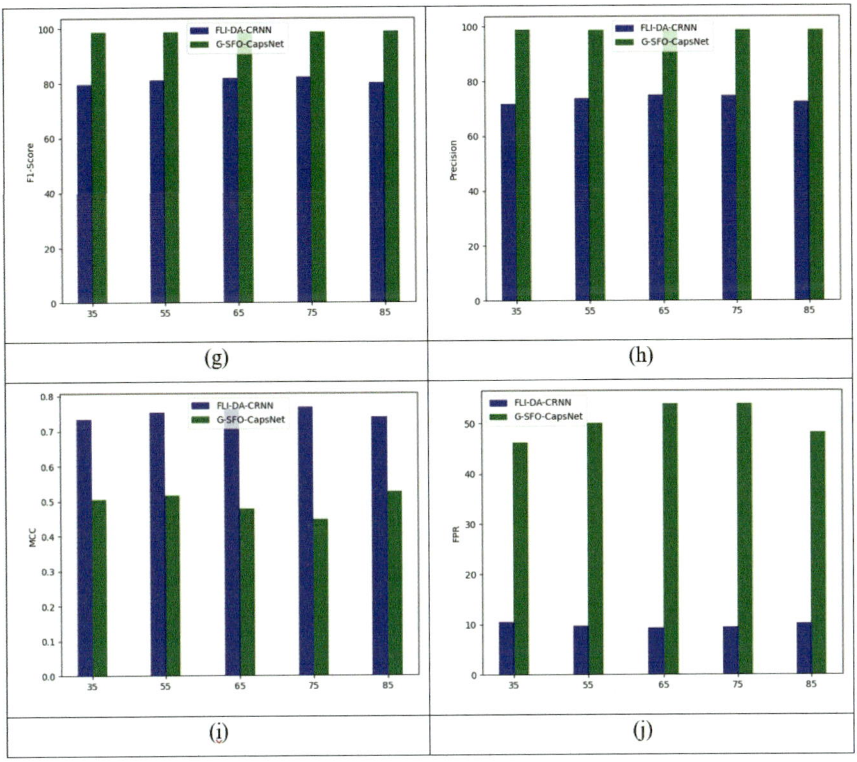

7.2.2 Comparative analysis of Dataset 2

The effectiveness analysis in terms of various performance measures among FLI-DA- CRNN and G-SFO-capsnet-based email spam detection approaches are given in Figure 7.2. The second contribution G-SFO-capsnet attained improved FNR, FPR and FDR of 82.52%, 96.29%, and 78.72% than G-SFO-capsnet-based email spam detection approach when considering the learning percentage value of 35. The overall plots revealed that the overall performance of the FLI-DA-CRNN-based email spam detection approach is higher than the G-SFO-capsnet-based email spam detection approach.

Figure 7.3: Continued.

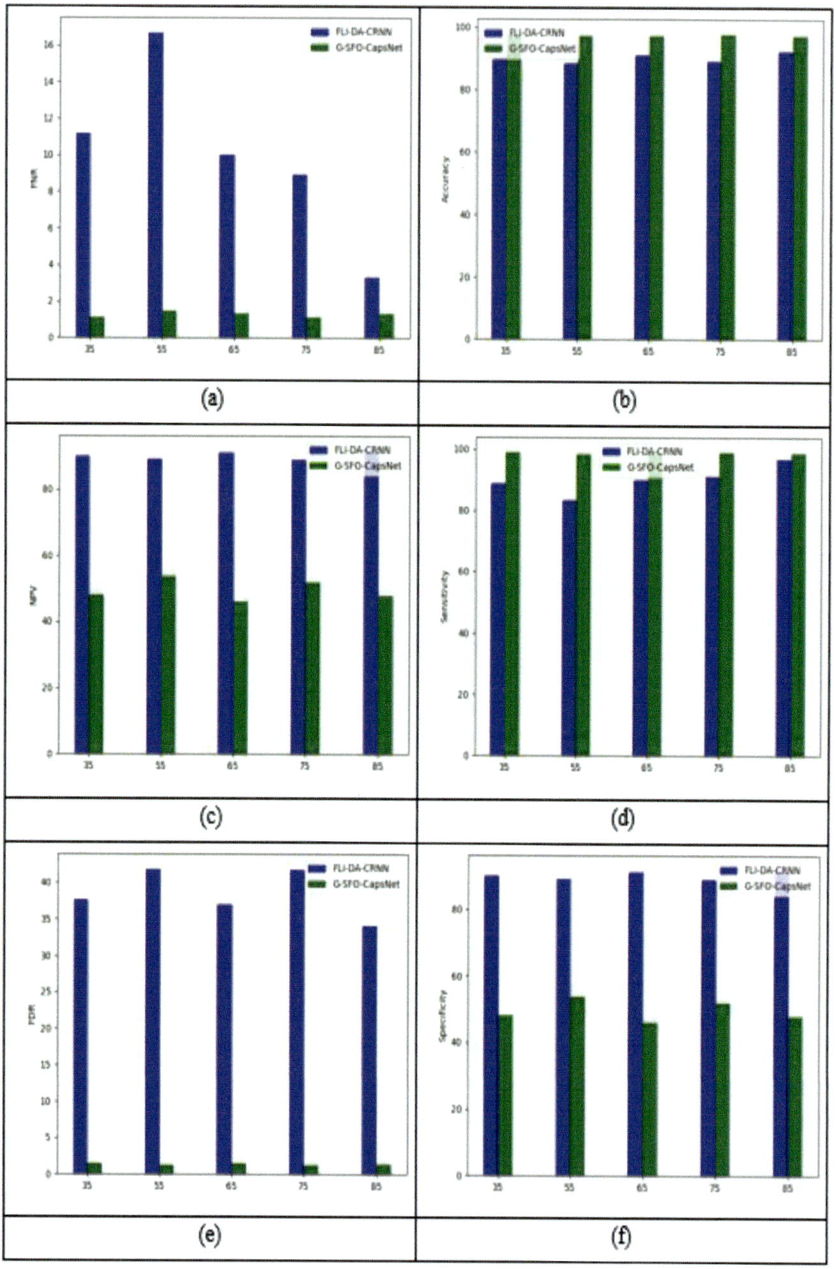

Figure 7.3: Performance computation among two different email spam detection approaches for Dataset 3 in regards to (a) FNR, (b) accuracy, (c) NPV, (d) sensitivity, (e) FDR, (f) specificity, (g) F1-score, (h) precision, (i) MCC, and (j) FPR.

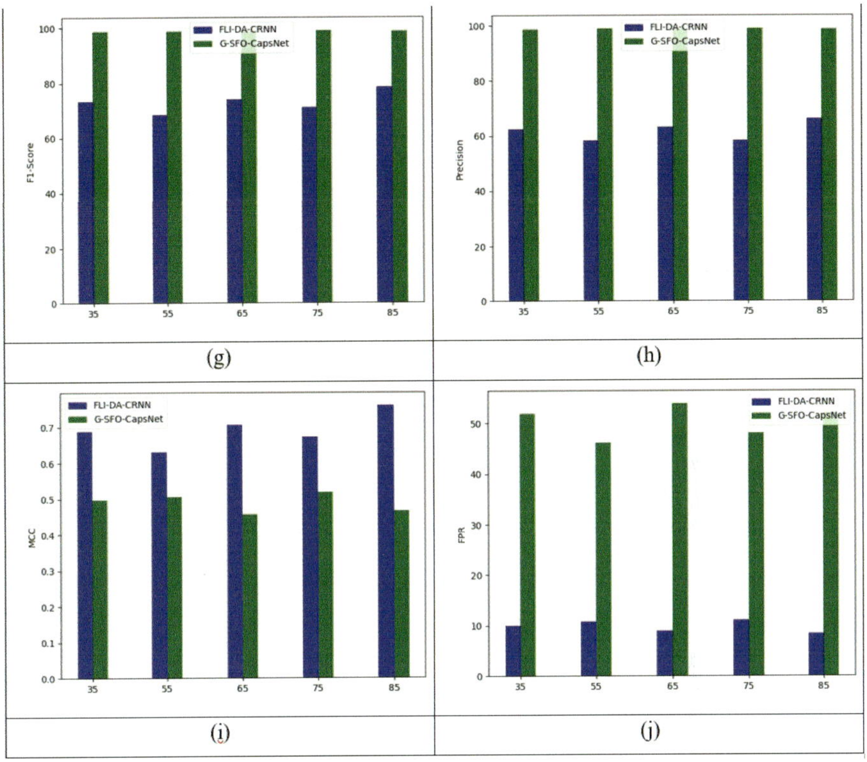

7.2.3 Comparative analysis of Dataset 3

The comparative analysis of the performance among two distinct email spam detection approaches with respect to Dataset 3 is given in Figure 7.3. The results depicted that the second contribution achieved enhanced FNR of 86.36%, Accuracy of 7.77%, NPV of 88.88%, Sensitivity of 10.36%, FDR of 94.44%, specificity of 51.72%, F1-score of 33.33%, precision of 59.01%, MCC of 90.47%, and FPR of 81.82% in accordance with the learning percentage value of 65. All the performance measures are attained with improved outcomes over the detection of email spam in the second contribution than the first contribution.

Figure 7.4: Continued.

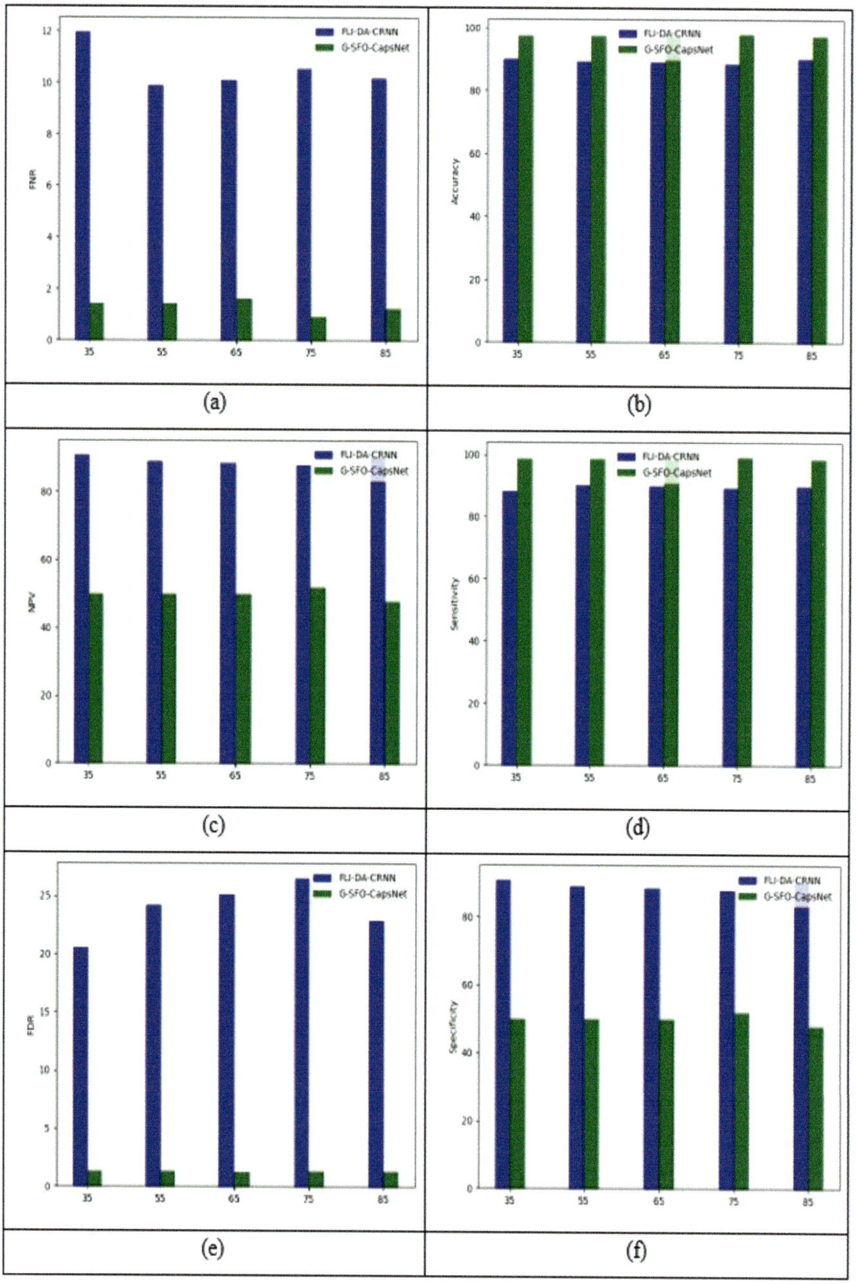

Figure 7.4: Performance computation among two different email spam detection approaches for Dataset 4 in regards to (a) FNR, (b) accuracy, (c) NPV, (d) sensitivity, (e) FDR, (f) specificity, (g) F1-score, (h) precision, (i) MCC, and (j) FPR.

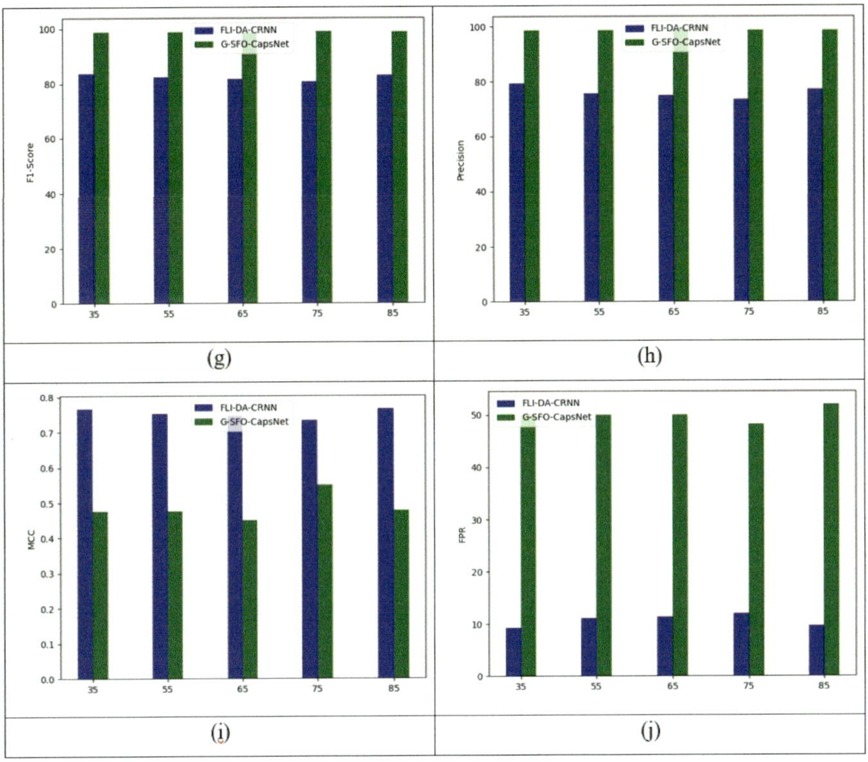

7.2.4 Comparative analysis of Dataset 4

The performance comparison among two different email spam detection approaches for Dataset 4 is illustrated in Figure 7.4. For considering the learning percentage value of 85, the second contribution obtained with enhanced FNR of 81.81%, accuracy of 6.59%, NPV of 84.78%, sensitivity of 12.94%, FDR of 91.81%, specificity of 42.52%, F1-score of 20.32%, precision of 22.78%, MCC of 60%, and FPR of 80. The effectiveness of the second contribution is greater than the first contribution for all the performance measures.

7.3 Summary

The developed G-SFO-capsnet-based email spam detection methodology attained better extensive performance than the FLI-DA-CRNN-based email spam detection approach, and it was verified through this comparative analysis. The second contribution proved its effectiveness among the four different datasets.

CHAPTER

8

Quantum Machine Learning for Email Spam Detection

8.1 Email Spam

Uninvited bulk email commonly known as spam refers to irrelevant or unwanted messages transmitted electronically, often for purposes such as advertising, phishing, or deploying malicious software. These messages, distributed at scale, are typically engineered to exploit communication systems for commercial gain or fraudulent intent.

As email has evolved into a primary channel for both corporate and personal interactions, the volume and sophistication of spam have increased markedly. These messages not only consume network resources and degrade user productivity but also pose significant cybersecurity threats, including malware propagation and identity theft.

In the early stages of digital communication, spam distribution was largely manual and unsophisticated. However, the expansion of the internet ecosystem and the rise of automated marketing tools led to the development of advanced spamming techniques. Modern spam operations employ tactics such as botnet distribution, sender spoofing, and payload obfuscation to evade traditional filtering mechanisms [130, 131].

In response to these advancements, the adoption of automated spam detection systems often incorporating machine learning and heuristic analysis has become critical for safeguarding communication infrastructure and maintaining information integrity.

DOI: 10.1201/9788743810384-8

8.2 Conventional Spam Detection Methods

8.2.1 Early rule-based methods

Initial spam detection methodologies predominantly relied on rule-based systems, wherein domain experts manually defined heuristic rules derived from empirical patterns observed in spam messages. For instance, the occurrence of specific lexical indicators such as "free," "money," or "offer" within the email subject line or body was often used as a basis for classification.

While these systems offered a straightforward implementation, they exhibited limited adaptability and scalability. Maintaining their effectiveness necessitated continuous manual rule updates in response to evolving spam strategies. Moreover, such systems were prone to significant classification errors, including high false positive rates where legitimate messages were incorrectly identified as spam and false negatives, wherein spam content evaded detection. These limitations underscored the need for more adaptive and intelligent filtering mechanisms [132].

8.2.2 Statistical models and machine learning

As spam tactics became increasingly sophisticated, traditional rule-based filtering methods proved inadequate, prompting a shift toward data-driven, statistical learning approaches. Machine learning techniques such as naïve Bayes classifiers, support vector machines (SVMs), and decision tree algorithms gained prominence in the domain of spam detection.

These models leverage various email features, including token frequency distributions, sender metadata, and header attributes, to perform binary classification of messages as spam or legitimate (ham). Unlike static rule-based systems, machine learning models possess the ability to generalize from training data, enabling dynamic adaptation to evolving spam characteristics.

For example, the naïve Bayes classifier applies Bayesian probability to compute the likelihood of an email being spam based on the presence and frequency of particular terms within the message. In contrast, SVMs aim to construct an optimal separating hyperplane in a high-dimensional feature space that maximally distinguishes between spam and non-spam instances. The transition to these statistical techniques marked a significant advancement in the robustness and scalability of spam filtering systems.

8.3 Limitations of Conventional Methods

8.3.1 Scalability problems

The rapid growth in email traffic introduced significant scalability challenges for traditional spam detection systems. As feature sets expanded to enhance classification accuracy, the computational complexity of the underlying algorithms also increased, resulting in slower processing times and higher resource consumption.

Moreover, the presence of large-scale datasets further exacerbated these issues by substantially prolonging model training durations. This posed a critical bottleneck for real-time email filtering applications, where low-latency response is essential for maintaining system performance and user experience.

8.3.2 Dimensionality issue

Spam detection algorithms frequently operate in high-dimensional feature spaces, incorporating a diverse range of attributes such as lexical tokens, user behavior patterns, and message metadata. As the dimensionality of the feature space increases, these models become susceptible to the curse of dimensionality, a phenomenon in which the computational complexity and sparsity of the data grow exponentially.

This increased complexity hinders the efficient extraction of discriminative patterns and complicates the feature selection process. Consequently, the model's capacity to generalize effectively to previously unseen emails may degrade, leading to reduced detection accuracy and increased risk of overfitting.

8.3.3 Computational inade quacies

Traditional spam detection systems incur substantial computational overhead, necessitating extensive memory and processing resources to manage large-scale datasets and perform model training. Even contemporary machine learning paradigms, including deep learning architectures, encounter scalability constraints when operating on massive, high-dimensional input spaces, often resulting in inefficiencies related to training time and inference latency.

These limitations have driven interest in alternative computational frameworks capable of addressing such bottlenecks. In particular, quantum computing has emerged as a promising avenue, offering the potential for exponential speedups in data processing and optimization tasks relevant to spam detection.

8.4 Quantum Machine Learning in Spam Detection

By exploiting the fundamental principles of quantum mechanics, quantum machine learning enhances and accelerates traditional machine learning methods that run on classical computers. The design of quantum computers relies on leveraging quantum phenomena such as superposition and entanglement that often defy classical intuition.

These quantum devices can encode and process information on an exponential scale, surpassing the capabilities of conventional computing hardware, including tablets, smartphones, and even state-of-the-art supercomputers. This exponential information processing capacity positions quantum computing as a powerful tool for tackling complex computational challenges.

Quantum machine learning (QML) integrates algorithms designed for execution on quantum hardware such as quantum computers to enhance and accelerate processes traditionally handled by classical machine learning systems. This approach, often termed quantum-enhanced machine learning, leverages the advanced information processing capabilities of quantum technologies to improve the efficiency of model training and inference.

Unlike classical computers, which face inherent limitations in storage and computational speed, quantum computing platforms utilize phenomena like superposition and entanglement to achieve exponential growth in both memory capacity and processing power. This enables the efficient handling and analysis of extensive datasets that would be computationally intensive or infeasible for classical systems.

By exploiting this expanded computational capability, quantum machine learning expedites the development and refinement of various machine learning architectures, including neural networks and other artificial intelligence models, ultimately driving improvements in both speed and performance [133].

8.4.1 Quantum speedup

Quantum computing promises exponential speedup over classical computers in specific problems, such as optimization, search, and classification. Quantum algorithms can process and analyze high- dimensional data much faster by exploiting phenomena like superposition and entanglement. For spam detection, quantum machine learning could enable real-time processing of emails and more efficient handling of large-scale datasets [134].

8.4.2 Addressing feature and data complexity

Quantum machine learning offers an inherent advantage in managing high-dimensional data. Unlike classical computers, which must process large datasets sequentially, quantum computers can analyze multiple possible outcomes at once, potentially identifying patterns in spam detection more efficiently. By utilizing quantum circuits for feature extraction and classification, quantum algorithms can overcome the complexity and resource limitations of classical methods (Table 8.1).

8.5 Conventional Machine Learning Techniques for Spam Detection

Email is a widely utilized digital communication medium that facilitates broad and efficient information dissemination. Emails can be categorized into two primary types: legitimate (ham) email and unsolicited (spam) email. Spam emails are typically characterized by their bulk delivery and unsolicited nature. These messages often serve as vectors for advertising content, phishing attempts, and the distribution of malicious software, including malware, Trojans, and other forms of harmful payloads.

8.5.1 Supervised learning methods for spam detection

8.5.1.1 Support vector machines (SVMs)

Support vector machines (SVMs) are a class of supervised learning algorithms used for classification tasks. In spam detection, SVMs work by mapping email features into a higher- dimensional space using a kernel function. The goal is to find a hyperplane that separates spam emails from non-spam emails with maximum margin. SVMs are effective at handling high- dimensional feature spaces, making them suitable for spam classification when combined with feature extraction methods such as TF-IDF or word embeddings.

Table 8.1: Summary of machine learning algorithms employed in previous research on email spam detection, along with the classifier that reported the best accuracy for each study.

Paper no.	Machine learning classifiers used	Classifier with best accuracy
[130]	Naïve Bayes, k-nearest neighbors, artificial neural network, support vector machine	Artificial neural network (98.5%)
[131]	Naïve Bayes, J48, multi-layer perceptron	Multi-layer perceptron (99.3%)
[132]	Naïve Bayes, SVM, C4.5, Adaboost C4.5, bagging C4.5, random forests, logistic regression, rough sets	Rough sets (99.4%)
[133]	C4.5, CART, REP tree, LAD tree, NB tree, random forest, rotation forest	Random forest (95.80%)
[134]	Naïve Bayes, support vector machine	Naïve Bayes (99.49%)
[135]	Naïve Bayes, support vector machine	Support vector machine (99%)
[136]	Decision trees, k-nearest neighbor, Bayesian networks, random forest, support vector machine, multi-layer perceptron	Random forest (97.69%)
[137]	Bayesian Logistic regression, hidden Naïve Bayes, rotation forest (94.2%) RBF network, voted perceptron, lazy Bayesian Rule, Logit Boost, rotation forest, NNge, logistic model tree, REP tree, naïve Bayes, J48, multilayer perceptron, random tree	Rotation forest (94.2%)
[138]	Artificial neural network, support vector machine, random forest	Random forest (99.93%)
[139]	Logistic regression, naïve Bayes, support vector neural network machine, neural network	Random forest (97.69%)
[140]	k-nearest neighbor, naïve Bayes, decision tree, support vector machine, random forest, logistic regression	Naïve Bayes, logistic regression (99%)
[141]	Artificial Neural network, Bayes classifier, decision table, k-nearest neighbor, logistic regression, naïve Bayes, radial basis function, random tree, random forest, support vector machine	Random forest (95.46%)

8.5.1.2 Naïve Bayes classifier

The naïve Bayes classifier is based on Bayes' theorem, which computes the probability of an email being spam given its content. The classifier assumes that the features (e.g., words in the email) are conditionally independent, which simplifies computation. Despite this simplifying assumption, naïve Bayes has proven to be highly effective in spam detection tasks, especially in scenarios where the dataset is large but sparse.

8.5.1.3 Decision trees and random forests

Decision trees are another classical method used in spam detection. These trees split the feature space into distinct regions based on the values of input features, and each leaf node represents a classification (spam or non-spam). Random forests, an ensemble method, combine multiple decision trees to reduce the overfitting problem. This increases the model's robustness and accuracy when classifying spam emails.

8.5.1.4 Deep neural networks (DNNs)

Deep learning, specifically deep neural networks (DNNs), is increasingly used for spam detection, especially when dealing with unstructured data such as email content. DNNs automatically learn patterns in data without requiring feature extraction. They are composed of multiple layers of neurons that progressively extract higher-level representations of the input data. Despite their effectiveness, DNNs can be computationally expensive and require large amounts of labeled data to perform well.

8.5.2 Feature extraction in spam detection

8.5.2.1 Text features

Textual features form the core of most spam detection systems. The most common text-based feature extraction methods include:

- Bag-of-words (BoW): This method represents each email as a vector of word counts. While simple, BoW often fails to capture word order and semantic relationships.

- Term frequency-inverse document frequency (TF-IDF): TF-IDF weighs words based on their frequency within a document and their rarity across the entire corpus. It helps capture more meaningful words in spam detection.
- Word embeddings (Word2Vec, GloVe): These models represent words as dense vectors in a continuous vector space, capturing semantic relationships. By embedding words into a lower-dimensional space, these techniques improve the ability to model the meanings behind words and phrases.

8.5.2.2 Metadata features

In addition to text-based features, metadata such as the email's sender, recipient, subject line, and timestamp can provide critical information. Features like the presence of attachments or unusual time patterns (e.g., emails sent at odd hours) can indicate spam. These features can be combined with text-based features to improve model performance.

8.5.2.3 User behavioral features

User-specific features, such as marking emails as spam or interacting with certain types of emails, help refine the spam detection process. These behavioral patterns can be incorporated into a model to personalize the detection process. For instance, if a user frequently marks emails from a specific sender as spam, the system can learn this preference and adapt its filtering [136].

8.6 Fundamentals of Quantum Computing: Key Concepts

8.6.1 Qubits and superposition

Quantum computing is based on qubits, which are analogous to classical bits but can represent both 0 and 1 simultaneously through a property called superposition. Superposition allows quantum computers to process multiple possibilities at once, enabling faster computation of certain problems. For spam detection, this could mean the ability to analyze a larger number of email features in parallel, drastically reducing processing time.

8.6.2 Quantum entanglement

Entanglement is a phenomenon where two qubits become correlated in such a way that the state of one qubit immediately affects the state of the other, even if they are far apart. Entanglement could be used in spam detection to link features of emails in a complex, interdependent manner, improving the classification process by capturing relationships that are difficult to model classically.

8.6.3 Quantum interference

Quantum interference allows quantum algorithms to amplify correct solutions while canceling out incorrect ones. In the context of spam detection, quantum interference could enable the classification of spam messages more efficiently by strengthening the correct classification paths while diminishing erroneous classifications.

8.6.4 Quantum gates and circuits

Quantum gates are operations applied to qubits to manipulate their states. Quantum circuits, consisting of sequences of quantum gates, are used to implement quantum algorithms. These circuits are the quantum analogs of classical machine learning algorithms. In spam detection, quantum circuits could be designed to transform classical features into quantum states that are easier to classify.

8.6.4.1 Pauli gates

Pauli gates are fundamental single-qubit gates used in quantum algorithms to perform operations like flipping the qubit's state. These gates play a critical role in quantum algorithms, including those that could be applied to spam detection.

8.6.4.2 Hadamard gate

The Hadamard gate creates superposition, an essential aspect of quantum parallelism. It is used in algorithms like Grover's search and can help process multiple email features simultaneously during spam classification tasks.

8.6.4.3 CNOT gate and controlled operations

The CNOT gate, or controlled NOT gate, is a two-qubit operation that performs a NOT operation on the second qubit only when the first qubit is in a specific state. This gate is fundamental for creating entanglement and is widely used in quantum algorithms.

8.6.5 Quantum measurement

Quantum measurement is a process that collapses a qubit's superposition into one of its basis states. The measurement process is probabilistic, and multiple measurements may be needed to determine the outcome with high confidence. In spam detection, quantum measurements can be used to determine whether an email is spam or not based on its quantum representation.

8.7 Quantum Machine Learning Algorithms for Spam Detection

8.7.1 Quantum support vector machines (QSVMs)

8.7.1.1 Quantum feature maps

Quantum feature maps are used to encode classical data (such as email features) into quantum states. This encoding allows quantum computers to perform operations on high-dimensional data more efficiently than classical systems. Quantum feature maps enable QSVMs to classify emails with improved accuracy and speed by taking advantage of quantum parallelism.

8.7.1.2 Speedup with quantum kernels

Quantum kernels are essential components of QSVMs. They enable the efficient computation of inner products in high-dimensional feature spaces, allowing QSVMs to identify spam patterns with far less computational cost than classical SVMs. This quantum speedup makes QSVMs a promising candidate for spam classification.

8.7.2 Quantum k-nearest neighbors (QkNN)

8.7.2.1 Quantum distance computation

In classical k-NN, the distance between data points is calculated to find the nearest neighbors. Quantum computing can dramatically speed up this distance calculation by leveraging quantum algorithms to compute distances more efficiently. This leads to faster and more accurate identification of spam emails.

8.7.2.2 Advantages over classical k-NN

Quantum k-NN offers several advantages, including exponential speedup in searching for the nearest neighbors in a high-dimensional space. This can significantly improve the efficiency of spam detection, especially when dealing with large datasets.

8.7.3 Quantum neural networks (QNNs)

8.7.3.1 Training quantum neural networks

Quantum neural networks are quantum circuits designed to perform machine learning tasks like classification and regression. In spam detection, QNNs can be used to identify intricate patterns in email content by using quantum gates to transform input features into quantum states that are easier to manipulate and classify.

8.7.3.2 High-dimensional data representation

QNNs can represent data in higher-dimensional quantum spaces, which is especially useful for spam detection tasks that involve complex and highly variable data. By leveraging quantum entanglement and superposition, QNNs can potentially identify hidden relationships between email features that are difficult to discern with classical methods.

8.7.4 Variational quantum algorithms (VQA)

8.7.4.1 Hybrid quantum-classical approaches

Variational quantum algorithms combine quantum circuits with classical optimization techniques. These hybrid algorithms are particularly effective for problems like spam detection, where quantum circuits can process high-dimensional data, and classical systems optimize the results.

8.7.4.2 Applications in spam detection

In spam detection, VQAs can improve the classification of emails by optimizing the parameters of quantum circuits, ensuring that the quantum classifier achieves the highest possible accuracy in identifying spam [138].

8.8 Challenges in Quantum Machine Learning for Spam Detection

8.8.1 Noisy intermediate-scale quantum (NISQ) devices

NISQ devices are currently the most widely available quantum computers, but they suffer from noise and errors that can limit their effectiveness in practical applications. For spam detection, these issues could reduce the reliability of quantum algorithms, especially when applied to real- world email datasets.

8.8.2 Quantum data encoding

Efficiently encoding classical data into quantum states remains a significant challenge. The way features are represented in quantum circuits can have a profound impact on the accuracy and efficiency of spam classification.

8.8.3 Scalability of quantum algorithms

Quantum machine learning algorithms often require large amounts of resources. Scaling them for large datasets, such as those encountered in email spam detection, presents a significant challenge due to the limited capabilities of current quantum hardware.

8.9 Future Directions in Quantum Machine Learning for Spam Detection

8.9.1 Advances in quantum hardware

As quantum hardware improves, with better error correction techniques and more stable qubits, quantum machine learning algorithms will become increasingly practical for tasks like spam detection.

8.9.2 Hybrid quantum-classical models

Combining quantum and classical systems in a hybrid model may offer the best of both worlds— leveraging the power of quantum algorithms for high-dimensional feature processing while maintaining the efficiency and reliability of classical systems for optimization and decision- making.

8.9.3 Quantum-enhanced feature extraction

Quantum computing could revolutionize feature extraction techniques by enabling more efficient identification of patterns and correlations in email data, improving the accuracy of spam classifiers.

8.10 Cybersecurity with Quantum Machine Learning

The integration of quantum computing and machine learning referred to as quantum machine learning (QML) holds significant promise due to the inherent synergies between the two paradigms. Both quantum computing and classical machine learning are fundamentally probabilistic in nature, a characteristic often viewed as a limitation but which, in this context, becomes a critical advantage.

Machine learning models inherently tolerate and even leverage uncertainty and approximation to process vast and complex datasets efficiently, enabling the extraction of patterns from high- dimensional, noisy, or ambiguously labeled data (e.g., image classification tasks where categorical boundaries such as "cat" vs. "dog" are not precisely defined). Quantum computing, characterized by superposition, entanglement, and probabilistic measurement, introduces computational frameworks capable of exponentially accelerating specific linear algebra operations central to many ML algorithms.

The alignment between the statistical framework of machine learning and the probabilistic nature of quantum mechanics facilitates the development of QML algorithms capable of handling complex inference and optimization problems beyond the capabilities of classical systems. Consequently, QML is positioned as one of the most promising early-stage, real-world applications of quantum computing, with the potential to transition from theoretical research into practical deployment across various domains [139].

The cybersecurity posture across the global digital infrastructure remains critically vulnerable. Both governmental institutions and private-sector organizations are increasingly challenged by a broad spectrum of sophisticated cyber threats, which continue to escalate in frequency, complexity, and impact. These threat vectors encompass advanced persistent threats (APTs) orchestrated by well-resourced and highly motivated adversaries, the proliferation of cybercrime-as-a-service (CaaS) platforms enabling commoditized malicious operations, and activities sponsored by nation- states. Such state-aligned operations include cyberterrorism, digital warfare tactics, and strategic industrial espionage, all of which target the confidentiality, integrity, and availability of critical systems and sensitive data.

Given the current maturity level of quantum computing technology, there is no immediate imperative for cybersecurity firms to formulate operational deployment strategies for quantum integration within near-term business workflows. However, the quantum ecosystem is progressing rapidly, marked by notable advancements such as Google's demonstration of a quantum error correction (QEC) protocol and IBM's release of the 433-qubit "Osprey" quantum processor. Concurrently, quantum research is transitioning from purely theoretical constructs to simulated implementations and, increasingly, to empirical experimentation on quantum hardware.

These developments signal a shift away from speculative discourse toward a more evidence-driven understanding of quantum computing's trajectory. The emergence of verifiable performance metrics and experimental data will soon enable more accurate forecasting of quantum capabilities and their practical timelines.

Strategic investment in quantum technologies necessitates a long-term vision, as immediate commercial or security-related returns remain limited. Nonetheless, deferring engagement until quantum solutions become mainstream carries significant risk. Organizations that fail to anticipate and prepare for the post-quantum paradigm may find themselves critically disadvantaged, particularly in areas such as cryptographic agility and quantum-resistant security architecture. The anticipated disruption will favor early adopters and may severely impact those that remain reactive rather than proactive.

Integration of cybersecurity and QML has benefits in many ways, as depicted in Figure 8.1. It is beneficial in anomaly detection, threat detection and response, data encryption and decryption, cyber threat detection, email spam detection and optimization in security protocols, and defense strategies.

Figure 8.1: Cybersecurity with QML.

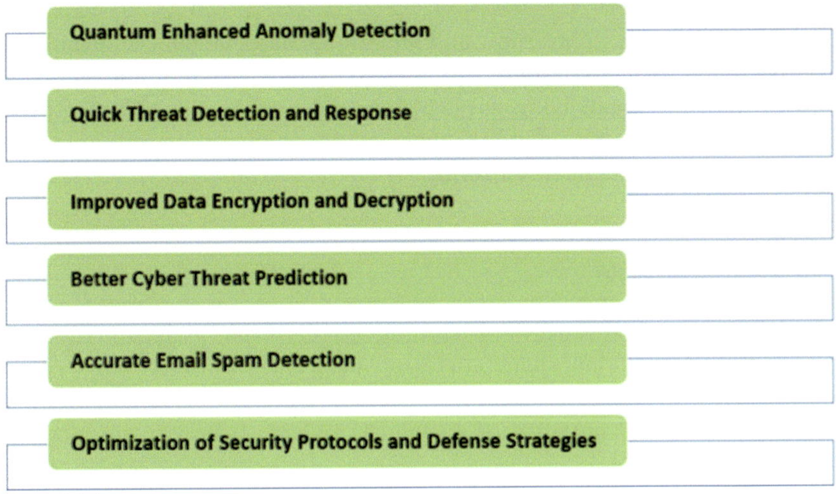

8.10.1 QML for email spam detection

The critical issues to be considered are spam message detection, malware detection, and security based on user behavior analysis on network traffic data. Email spam detection has been the critical issue in cyber security for a long time. Many email service providers have already provided the service with built in spam detection functionalities.

8.10.2 Significant practices in spam email

8.10.2.1 Detection email filtering

Email filtering is a foundational approach to identifying and managing spam. This method categorizes incoming emails into spam and legitimate (ham) categories. Modern filtering systems often leverage machine learning algorithms, which learn from historical data to recognize patterns in email content, headers, and metadata, such as sender reputation, subject line, and time of receipt.

8.10.2.2 Natural language processing (NLP)

NLP enables systems to interpret and analyze human language in emails. In spam detection, NLP techniques are used to extract semantic and syntactic features from the email body, subject line, and attachments. This helps in understanding the intent behind the message, identifying spammy phrases, or detecting deceptive language patterns.

8.10.2.3 Text classification

Text classification is a supervised learning approach that assigns predefined labels (e.g., "spam" or "not spam") to textual data. Algorithms like naïve Bayes, support vector machines (SVMs), and decision trees are commonly used to classify emails based on keyword frequency, stylistic features, and message structure.

8.10.2.4 Feature engineering

Effective spam detection relies heavily on the quality of features used in training models. Feature engineering involves extracting and selecting significant attributes such as the sender's domain, frequency of suspicious keywords, HTML usage, or email length. These features help algorithms distinguish between spam and legitimate messages more accurately.

8.10.2.5 Supervised learning

In this approach, the model is trained using a dataset of labeled emails. Each email is tagged as spam or not spam, allowing the model to learn the relationship between features and labels. Once trained, the model can classify new, unseen emails with high accuracy.

8.10.2.6 Unsupervised learning

Unlike supervised methods, unsupervised learning does not rely on labeled data. Instead, it identifies hidden patterns or structures within the email dataset. Techniques like clustering (e.g., K-means) or anomaly detection can be used to detect outliers that may indicate spam without prior labeling.

8.10.2.7 Deep learning

Deep learning techniques, especially convolutional neural networks (CNNs) and recurrent neural networks (RNNs), can automatically learn complex and abstract features from raw email data. These models are particularly effective when dealing with large volumes of data and have shown strong performance in detecting evasive or obfuscated spam content.

8.10.2.8 Neural networks

Neural networks simulate the structure of the human brain to recognize intricate patterns in data. In the context of spam detection, they can process text sequences, metadata, and contextual cues to accurately predict whether an email is spam. Advanced architectures like transformers (e.g., BERT) further enhance the model's ability to understand language nuances.

8.10.3 Email spam detection research

Spam is defined as unsolicited commercial electronic mail (UCE) directed at recipients with whom the sender has no pre-existing business or personal relationship, and which has not been sent with the explicit consent of the recipient. Commercial electronic mail (CEM) refers to any email where the primary objective is the advertisement or promotion of products or services. Spam typically encompasses unsolicited advertisements, business proposals, requests for favors, invitations to participate in charitable activities, or financial offers. Furthermore, spam is often used for more malicious purposes, such as phishing, a deceptive practice where attackers impersonate legitimate entities to coerce individuals into disclosing sensitive information, such as banking credentials or account details [140, 141].

In their research, the authors of [130] broaden the scope of spam to include content posted and distributed via platforms such as social media networks, product review websites, or in comments on blogs and microblogs, as well as video or status update sites. These forms of communication, commonly referred to as social media spam, are typically propagated by automated bots that generate accounts to distribute fraudulent content. According to Thomas et al., spammers are not limited to fraudulent profit-driven activities but also engage in spreading disinformation or conducting attacks aimed at censorship, particularly targeting political discourse.

Lau et al. [132] focus on the issue of spam within the context of fake reviews. They analyze datasets from a prominent e-commerce platform, investigating the potential of text mining techniques to detect fraudulent online reviews. Distinguishing between spam (fake reviews) and ham (genuine reviews) presents a significant challenge, as fake reviews are deliberately crafted to appear authentic and often written by humans, rather than generated through automated processes.

Hayati et al. [133] introduce the concept of "Spam 2.0", which refers to spambots that actively search for vulnerabilities within web platforms to exploit them for distributing spam content in subsequent stages. These advanced spamming techniques target websites, forums, and other online services, leveraging security loopholes for malicious purposes.

Dada et al. [135] provide an extensive systematic review of spam filtering techniques, including a survey of many research papers on the application of machine learning (ML) for spam filtering. Their research examines how leading service providers, such as Google, Yahoo, and Microsoft, employ ML techniques to filter spam emails.

8.11 Summary

Quantum machine learning (QML) presents a transformative opportunity in the domain of spam detection by enabling significantly faster data processing and enhanced capability to manage high- dimensional feature spaces. These advantages could surpass many of the inherent limitations of classical machine learning algorithms, particularly in terms of computational complexity and data representation efficiency.

Despite its promise, the practical deployment of QML in spam detection faces considerable challenges. Key obstacles include the current limitations of quantum hardware (e.g., qubit coherence, error rates), efficient quantum data encoding schemes, and issues related to algorithmic scalability. However, as quantum technologies mature and these technical barriers are progressively addressed, QML-based spam detection systems could evolve into a highly effective solution for identifying and mitigating unsolicited emails at scale.

CHAPTER

9

Conclusions and Future Scope

9.1 Conclusions

This research work on recommended automatic email spam detection models with deep learning approaches is concluded in this chapter. Three phases associated with the developed automated email spam filtering techniques have been elaborated. The first phase employed the TD-IDF technique to acquire the essential feature in a textural and visual format using correlogram and GLCM methods. Next, from the acquired features, optimal features were obtained by the FLI-DA technique. Later, the attained optimal features were subjected to an efficient email spam identification phase. Here, the fused combination with CNN and RNN model, and their parameters, like a hidden neuron in CNN and RNN, were optimized by the developed FLI-DA method to attain a better email spam detection rate. In the second phase, feature extraction was performed to obtain TV and TF-IDF features. Next, effective feature extraction was carried out by multiple techniques like WHT, FDA, and color correlograms to reduce the feature length. Here, the training complications were minimized by the G-SFO scheme and the adaptive capsule networks were employed to perform efficient spam detection in emails by the suggested G-SFO strategy to attain a better efficacy rate. The third stage of the developed model was the fused combination of existing email spam filtering models to attain an effectively higher spam prediction rate than the traditional techniques. Finally, the comparative framework secured an accurate spam recognition rate in emails than the conventional approaches in different observations.

DOI: 10.1201/9788743810384-9

9.2 Major Findings

The major findings associated with the implemented spam email identification models are elaborated as follows.

- In stage one, the suggested email spam detection framework secured a better efficacy rate than the classical approaches. Accuracy analysis performed on the FLI-DA-CRNN-based email spam identification method was 3.93% more efficient than DA-CRNN, 4.52% more effective than GWO-CRNN, 6.08% improved over PSO-CRNN, and 6.56% increased over WOA-CRNN with a learning rate of 85%. Moreover, the recommended technique obtained a better performance rate than the classical techniques in multiple performance measures.
- In stage two, the implemented G-SFO-capsnet-based email spam identification technique secured a better performance rate than the classical approaches as 1.5%, 1.22%, 1%, and 0.65% superior to GWO-capsnet, SFO-capsnet, WOA-capsnet, and PSO-capsnet, correspondingly at a learning rate of 55%. Thus, the initiated email spam detection framework has a better email spam recognition rate than the baseline techniques.
- In stage three, the fused framework is contrasted over different classical heuristic models and secured a better efficacy rate than the traditional schemes in different schemes. The implemented framework is contrasted using different measures like sensitivity, accuracy, specificity, precision, F1-score, and false positive metrics, and it attained a highly accurate performance rate in various experimental analyses over classical techniques.

9.3 Future Scope

Numerous prospects for future development within the proposed spam email detection systems are described below.

- Almost all researchers presented their results based on accuracy, precision, recall, etc., while the time complexity of machine learning models should be considered an evaluation metric.
- The email spam filtering models did not work effectively in the drift phenomenon concept, i.e. the nature of spam emails evolves over time and existing spam filtering models must be analyzed in near real time.
- The suggested framework could not handle the huge volume of emails in a real-world scenario.
- More image-based spam email identification filtering techniques are essential because the spammers forward the messages in the form of stego images to escape detection.
- The false positive rate of many models is still higher than required. It must be reduced to the smallest possible value in future.
- Real-time spam classification is much needed as most of the proposed models cannot work on real-time data.

- Labeled data is one of the major issues in spam detection. There are a few new labeled and up-to-date datasets for this purpose and thus there is a need to adopt standard data in future.
- Multilingual spam detection should be explored in the future.
- It is essential to design a system with high scalability, adaptability, and integration using semantic web patterns for effective spam email detection.
- Minimizing filters effectively reduce the efficacy of the network in the feature space.
- More processing layers and multi-level abstraction are essential to offer a better performance rate with deep structured architecture.

References

[1] J. Choi and C. Jeon, "Cost-Based Heterogeneous Learning Framework for Real- Time Spam Detection in Social Networks With Expert Decisions," IEEE Access, vol. 9, pp. 103573-103587, 2021,

[2] X. Liu, H. Lu and A. Nayak, "A Spam Transformer Model for SMS Spam Detection," IEEE Access, vol. 9, pp. 80253-80263, 2021.

[3] G. Lingam, R. R. Rout, D. V. L. N. Somayajulu and S. K. Ghosh, "Particle Swarm Optimization on Deep Reinforcement Learning for Detecting Social Spam Bots and Spam-Influential Users in Twitter Network," IEEE Systems Journal, vol. 15, no. 2, pp. 2281-2292, June 2021.

[4] Z. Zhang, R. Hou and J. Yang, "Detection of Social Network Spam Based on Improved Extreme Learning Machine," IEEE Access, vol. 8, pp. 112003-112014, 2020.

[5] H. Shen and Z. Li, "Leveraging Social Networks for Effective Spam Filtering," IEEE Transactions on Computers, vol. 63, no. 11, pp. 2743-2759, Nov. 2014.

[6] C. -Y. Tseng, P. -C. Sung and M. -S. Chen, "Cosdes: A Collaborative Spam Detection System with a Novel E-Mail Abstraction Scheme," IEEE Transactions on Knowledge and Data Engineering, vol. 23, no. 5, pp. 669-682, May 2011.

[7] S. Sedhai and A. Sun, "Semi-Supervised Spam Detection in Twitter Stream," IEEE Transactions on Computational Social Systems, vol. 5, no. 1, pp. 169-175, March 2018.

[8] Xin Tong; Jingya Wang; Changlin Zhang; Runzheng Wang; Zhilin Ge; Wenmao Liu; Zhiyan Zhao, "A Content-Based Chinese Spam Detection Method Using a Capsule Network With Long-Short Attention," IEEE Sensors Journal, vol. 21, no. 22, pp. 25409-25420, 15 Nov.15, 2021.

[9] T. Xia, "A Constant Time Complexity Spam Detection Algorithm for Boosting Throughput on Rule-Based Filtering Systems," IEEE Access, vol. 8, pp. 82653- 82661, 2020.

[10] Sanaa A. A. Ghaleb; Mumtazimah Mohamad; Waheed Ali H. M. Ghanem; Abdullah B. Nasser; Mohamed Ghetas, "Feature Selection by Multiobjective Optimization: Application to Spam Detection System by Neural Networks and Grasshopper Optimization Algorithm," IEEE Access, vol. 10, pp. 98475-98489, 2022.

[11] D. Liu and J. -H. Lee, "CNN Based Malicious Website Detection by Invalidating Multiple Web Spams," IEEE Access, vol. 8, pp. 97258-97266, 2020.

[12] X. Wang, Q. Kang, J. An and M. Zhou, "Drifted Twitter Spam Classification Using Multiscale Detection Test on K-L Divergence," IEEE Access, vol. 7, pp. 108384-108394, 2019.

[13] Chao Chen; Jun Zhang; Yi Xie; Yang Xiang; Wanlei Zhou; Mohammad Mehedi Hassan; Abdulhameed AlElaiwi; Majed, "A Performance Evaluation of Machine Learning-Based Streaming Spam Tweets Detection," IEEE Transactions on Computational Social Systems, vol. 2, no. 3, pp. 65-76, Sept. 2015.

[14] Tiantian Zhu; Hongyu Gao; Yi Yang; Kai Bu; Yan Chen; Doug Downey; Kathy Lee; Alok N. Choudhary, "Beating the Artificial Chaos: Fighting OSN Spam Using Its Own Templates," IEEE/ACM Transactions on Networking, vol. 24, no. 6, pp. 3856-3869, December 2016.

[15] A. AlMahmoud, E. Damiani, H. Otrok and Y. Al-Hammadi, "Spamdoop: A Privacy-Preserving Big Data Platform for Collaborative Spam Detection," IEEE Transactions on Big Data, vol. 5, no. 3, pp. 293-304, 1 Sept. 2019.

[16] E. Soares, C. Garcia, R. Poucas, H. Camargo and D. Leite, "Evolving Fuzzy Set-based and Cloud-based Unsupervised Classifiers for Spam Detection," IEEE Latin America Transactions, vol. 17, no. 09, pp. 1449-1457, September 2019.

[17] S. Shehnepoor, M. Salehi, R. Farahbakhsh and N. Crespi, "NetSpam: A Network-Based Spam Detection Framework for Reviews in Online Social Media," IEEE Transactions on Information Forensics and Security, vol. 12, no. 7, pp. 1585- 1595, July 2017.

[18] Z. Guo, K. Yu, A. Jolfaei, F. Ding and N. Zhang, "Fuz-Spam: Label Smoothing- Based Fuzzy Detection of Spammers in Internet of Things," IEEE Transactions on Fuzzy Systems, vol. 30, no. 11, pp. 4543-4554, Nov. 2022.

[19] G. Lin, N. Sun, S. Nepal, J. Zhang, Y. Xiang and H. Hassan, "Statistical Twitter Spam Detection Demystified: Performance, Stability and Scalability," IEEE Access, vol. 5, pp. 11142-11154, 2017.

[20] C. Chen, Y. Wang, J. Zhang, Y. Xiang, W. Zhou and G. Min, "Statistical Features-Based Real-Time Detection of Drifted Twitter Spam," IEEE

Transactions on Information Forensics and Security, vol. 12, no. 4, pp. 914-925, April 2017.

[21] S. Madisetty and M. S. Desarkar, "A Neural Network-Based Ensemble Approach for Spam Detection in Twitter," IEEE Transactions on Computational Social Systems, vol. 5, no. 4, pp. 973-984, Dec. 2018.

[22] H. Tajalizadeh and R. Boostani, "A Novel Stream Clustering Framework for Spam Detection in Twitter," IEEE Transactions on Computational Social Systems, vol. 6, no. 3, pp. 525-534, June 2019.

[23] L. Araujo and J. Martinez-Romo, "Web Spam Detection: New Classification Features Based on Qualified Link Analysis and Language Models," IEEE Transactions on Information Forensics and Security, vol. 5, no. 3, pp. 581-590, Sept. 2010.

[24] B. Halawi, A. Mourad, H. Otrok and E. Damiani, "Few are as Good as Many: An Ontology-Based Tweet Spam Detection Approach," IEEE Access, vol. 6, pp. 63890-63904, 2018.

[25] H. Oh, "A YouTube Spam Comments Detection Scheme Using Cascaded Ensemble Machine Learning Model," IEEE Access, vol. 9, pp. 144121-144128, 2021.

[26] L. Behan, J. Rozhon, J. Safarik, F. Rezac and M. Voznak, "Efficient Detection of Spam Over Internet Telephony by Machine Learning Algorithms," IEEE Access, vol. 10, pp. 133412-133426, 2022.

[27] Y. Tan, Q. Wang and G. Mi, "Ensemble Decision for Spam Detection Using Term Space Partition Approach," IEEE Transactions on Cybernetics, vol. 50, no. 1, pp. 297-309, Jan. 2020.

[28] M. A. Azad, S. Bag, S. Tabassum and F. Hao, "privy: Privacy Preserving Collaboration Across Multiple Service Providers to Combat Telecom Spams," IEEE Transactions on Emerging Topics in Computing, vol. 8, no. 2, pp. 313-327, 1 April- June 2020.

[29] A. Makkar, U. Ghosh and P. K. Sharma, "Artificial Intelligence and Edge Computing-Enabled Web Spam Detection for Next Generation IoT Applications," IEEE Sensors Journal, vol. 21, no. 22, pp. 25352-25361, 15 Nov.15, 2021.

[30] A. Makkar, S. Garg, N. Kumar, M. S. Hossain, A. Ghoneim and M. Alrashoud, "An Efficient Spam Detection Technique for IoT Devices Using Machine Learning," IEEE Transactions on Industrial Informatics, vol. 17, no. 2, pp. 903-912, Feb. 2021.

[31] K. Zhang, X. Liang, R. Lu and X. Shen, "PIF: A Personalized Fine-Grained Spam Filtering Scheme With Privacy Preservation in Mobile Social Networks," IEEE Transactions on Computational Social Systems, vol. 2, no. 3, pp. 41-52, Sept. 2015.

[32] I. L. d. Oliveira, J. L. Corrêa and A. M. Cansian, "Using the Euclidean Distance as a Mechanism Distance between Signatures to the Detect

Spam and Phishing Scams," IEEE Latin America Transactions, vol. 8, no. 4, pp. 340-348, Aug. 2010.

[33] Faiza Masood; Ghana Ammad; Ahmad Almogren; Assad Abbas; Hasan Ali Khattak; Ikram Ud Din; Mohsen Guiz, "Spammer Detection and Fake User Identification on Social Networks," IEEE Access, vol. 7, pp. 68140-68152, 2019.

[34] N. Ruan, Z. Wei and J. Liu, "Cooperative Fraud Detection Model With Privacy- Preserving in Real CDR Datasets," IEEE Access, vol. 7, pp. 115261-115272, 2019.

[35] J. Oh, G. -Y. Youm and M. Kim, "SPAM-Net: A CNN-Based SAR Target Recognition Network With Pose Angle Marginalization Learning," IEEE Transactions on Circuits and Systems for Video Technology, vol. 31, no. 2, pp. 701- 714, Feb. 2021.

[36] N. Hussain, H. Turab Mirza, I. Hussain, F. Iqbal and I. Memon, "Spam Review Detection Using the Linguistic and Spammer Behavioral Methods," IEEE Access, vol. 8, pp. 53801-53816, 2020.

[37] T. Qiu, H. Wang, K. Li, H. Ning, A. K. Sangaiah and B. Chen, "SIGMM: A Novel Machine Learning Algorithm for Spammer Identification in Industrial Mobile Cloud Computing," IEEE Transactions on Industrial Informatics, vol. 15, no. 4, pp. 2349-2359, April 2019.

[38] Zhiwei Guo; Yu Shen; Ali Kashif Bashir; Muhammad Imran; Neeraj Kumar; Di Zhang; Keping Yu, "Robust Spammer Detection Using Collaborative Neural Network in Internet-of-Things Applications," IEEE Internet of Things Journal, vol. 8, no. 12, pp. 9549-9558, 15 June15, 2021.

[39] G. Al-Rawashdeh, R. Mamat and N. Hafhizah Binti Abd Rahim, "Hybrid Water Cycle Optimization Algorithm With Simulated Annealing for Spam E-mail Detection," IEEE Access, vol. 7, pp. 143721-143734, 2019.

[40] E. Ezpeleta, U. Zurutuza and J. M. G. Hidalgo, "A study of the personalization of spam content using Facebook public information," Logic Journal of the IGPL, vol. 25, no. 1, pp. 30-41, Feb. 2017.

[41] P. Rajendran, A. Tamilarasi and R. Mynavathi, "A Collaborative Abstraction Based Email Spam Filtering with Fingerprints," Wireless Personal Communications, vol.123, pp.1913–1923, 2022.

[42] Maryam Shuaib, Shafi'i Muhammad Abdulhamid, Olawale Surajudeen Adebayo, Oluwafemi Osho, Ismaila Idris, John K. Alhassan and Nadim Rana, "Whale optimization algorithm-based email spam feature selection method using rotation forest algorithm for classification," SN Applied Sciences, vol.1, 2019.

[43] Rozita Talaei Pashiri, Yaser Rostami and Mohsen Mahrami, "Spam detection through feature selection using artificial neural network and sine–cosine algorithm," Mathematical Sciences, vol.14, pp.193–199, 2020.

[44] Ali Hosseinalipour and Reza Ghanbarzadeh, "A novel approach for spam detection using horse herd optimization algorithm," Neural Computing and Applications, vol.34, pp.13091–13105, 2022.

[45] T. Kumaresan, S. Saravanakumar and R. Balamurugan, "Visual and textual features based email spam classification using S-Cuckoo search and hybrid kernel support vector machine," Cluster Computing, vol.22, pp.33–46, 2019.

[46] Furqan Rustam, Najia Saher, Arif Mehmood, Ernesto Lee, Sandrilla Washington and Imran Ashraf, "Detecting ham and spam emails using feature union and supervised machine learning models," Multimedia Tools and Applications, 2023.

[47] Yeqin Shao, Marcello Trovati, Quan Shi, Olga Angelopoulou, Eleana Asimakopoulou and Nik Bessis, "A hybrid spam detection method based on unstructured datasets," Soft Computing, vol.21, pp.233–243, 2017.

[48] Devottam Gaurav, Sanju Mishra Tiwari, Ayush Goyal, Niketa Gandhi and Ajith Abraham, "Machine intelligence-based algorithms for spam filtering on document labeling," Soft Computing, vol.24, pp.9625–9638, 2020.

[49] Muhammad Hassan Arif, Jianxin Li, Muhammad Iqbal and Kaixu Liu, "Sentiment analysis and spam detection in short informal text using learning classifier systems," Soft Computing, vol.22, pp.7281–7291, 2018.

[50] Gauri Jain, Manisha Sharma and Basant Agarwal, "Spam detection in social media using convolutional and long short term memory neural network," Annals of Mathematics and Artificial Intelligence, vol.85, pp.21–44, 2019.

[51] Guangchen Ruan and Ying Tan, "A three-layer back-propagation neural network for spam detection using artificial immune concentration," Soft Computing, vol.14, pp.139–150, 2010.

[52] Bin Wang, Gareth J. F. Jones and Wenfeng Pan, "Using online linear classifiers to filter spam emails," Pattern Analysis and Applications, vol.9, pp.339–351, 2006.

[53] Poria Pirozmand, Mehdi Sadeghilalimi, Ali Asghar Rahmani Hosseinabadi, Fatemeh Sadeghilalimi, Seyedsaeid Mirkamali and Adam Slowik, "A feature selection approach for spam detection in social networks using gravitational force- based heuristic algorithm," Journal of Ambient Intelligence and Humanized Computing, vol.14, pp.1633–1646, 2023.

[54] S. Sumathi and Ganesh Kumar Pugalendhi, "RETRACTED ARTICLE: Cognition based spam mail text analysis using combined approach of deep neural network classifier and random forest," Journal of Ambient Intelligence and Humanized Computing, vol.12, pp.5721–5731, 2021.

[55] Mai A. Shaaban, Yasser F. Hassan and Shawkat K. Guirguis, "Deep convolutional forest: a dynamic deep ensemble approach for spam detection in text," Complex & Intelligent Systems, vol.8, pp.4897–4909, 2022.

[56] Juan Carlos Gomez, Erik Boiy and Marie-Francine Moens, "Highly discriminative statistical features for email classification," Knowledge and Information Systems, vol.31, pp.23–53, 2012.

[57] Ioannis Katakis, Grigorios Tsoumakas and Ioannis Vlahavas, "Tracking recurring contexts using ensemble classifiers: an application to email filtering," Knowledge and Information Systems, vol.22, pp.371–391, 2010.

[58] Priyatam Naravajhula and Alekhya Naravajula, "Spam Classification: Genetically Optimized Passive-Aggressive Approach," SN Computer Science, vol.4, 2023.

[59] Xianghan Zheng, Xueying Zhang, Yuanlong Yu, Tahar Kechadi and Chunming Rong, "ELM-based spammer detection in social networks," The Journal of Supercomputing, vol.72, pp.2991–3005, 2016.

[60] Teena Jose and Suvanam Sasidhar Babu, "Detecting spammers on social network through clustering technique," Journal of Ambient Intelligence and Humanized Computing, 2019.

[61] Haiying Shen, and ze li "Leveraging Social Networks for Effective Spam Filtering,"IEEE Transactions on Computers, vol. 63, no. 11, pp. 2743-2759, November 2014.

[62] G. Al-Rawashdeh, R. Mamat and N. Hafhizah Binti Abd Rahim, "Hybrid Water Cycle Optimization Algorithm With Simulated Annealing for Spam E-mail Detection," IEEE Access, vol. 7, pp. 143721-143734, 2019.

[63] A. Karim, S. Azam, B. Shanmugam and K. Kannoorpatti, "An Unsupervised Approach for Content-Based Clustering of Emails Into Spam and Ham Through Multiangular Feature Formulation," IEEE Access, vol. 9, pp. 135186-135209, 2021.

[64] S. A. A. Ghaleb et al., "Feature Selection by Multiobjective Optimization: Application to Spam Detection System by Neural Networks and Grasshopper Optimization Algorithm," IEEE Access, vol. 10, pp. 98475-98489, 2022.

[65] S. A. A. Ghaleb, M. Mohamad, S. A. Fadzli and W. A. H. M. Ghanem, "Training Neural Networks by Enhance Grasshopper Optimization Algorithm for Spam Detection System," IEEE Access, vol. 9, pp. 116768-116813, 2021.

[66] S. Gibson, B. Issac, L. Zhang and S. M. Jacob, "Detecting Spam Email With Machine Learning Optimized With Bio-Inspired Metaheuristic Algorithms," IEEE Access, vol. 8, pp. 187914-187932, 2020.

[67] Isra'a AbdulNabi, and Qussai Yaseen,"Spam Email Detection Using Deep Learning Techniques,"Procedia Computer Science, Vol. 184, pp. 853-858, 2021.

[68] Ismaila Idris, Ali Selamat, Ngoc Thanh Nguyen, Sigeru Omatu, Ondrej Krejcar, Kamil Kuca, and Marek Penhaker, "A combined negative selection algorithm– particle swarm optimization for an email spam detection system," Engineering Applications of Artificial Intelligence, Vol. 39, pp. 33-44, March 2015.

[69] Amany A. Naem, Neveen I. Ghali, and Afaf A. Saleh,"Antlion optimization and boosting classifier for spam email detection,"Future Computing and Informatics Journal, Vol. 3, Issue 2, pp. 436-442, December 2018.

[70] Ismaila Idris, and Ali Selamat,"Improved email spam detection model with negative selection algorithm and particle swarm optimization,"Applied Soft Computing, Vol. 22, pp. 11-27, September 2014.

[71] Francisco Jáñez-Martino, Rocío Alaiz-Rodríguez, Víctor González-Castro, Eduardo Fidalgo, and Enrique Alegre,"Classifying spam emails using agglomerative hierarchical clustering and a topic-based approach,"Applied Soft Computing, Vol. 139, no. 110226, May 2023.

[72] Clotilde Lopes, Paulo Cortez, Pedro Sousa, Miguel Rocha, and Miguel Rio,"Symbiotic filtering for spam email detection,"Expert Systems with Applications, Vol. 38, Issue 8, pp. 9365-9372, August 2011.

[73] Ismaila Idris, Ali Selamat, and Sigeru Omatu,"Hybrid email spam detection model with negative selection algorithm and differential evolution,"Engineering Applications of Artificial Intelligence, Vol. 28, pp. 97-110, February 2014.

[74] Ashraf S. Mashaleh, Noor Farizah Binti Ibrahim, Mohammed Azmi Al-Betar, Hossam M.J. Mustafa, and Qussai M. Yaseen,"Detecting Spam Email with Machine Learning Optimized with Harris Hawks optimizer (HHO) Algorithm,"Procedia Computer Science, Vol. 201, pp. 659-664, 2022.

[75] Chanchal Kumar, Taran Singh Bharti, and Shiv Prakash,"A hybrid Data-Driven framework for Spam detection in Online Social Network,"Procedia Computer Science, Vol. 218, pp. 124-132, 2023.

[76] Safaa Magdy, Yasmine Abouelseoud, and Mervat Mikhail,"Efficient spam and phishing emails filtering based on deep learning," Computer Networks, Vol. 206, no. 108826, 7 April 2022.

[77] N. Mageshkumar, A. Vijayaraj, N. Arunpriya, and A. Sangeetha,"Efficient spam filtering through intelligent text modification detection using machine learning," Materials Today: Proceedings, vol. 64. no. 11, May 2022.

[78] Melvin Diale, Turgay Celik, and Christiaan Van Der Walt, "Unsupervised feature learning for spam email filtering," Computers & Electrical Engineering, vol. 74, pp. 89-104, March 2019.

[79] U. Murugavel, and R. Santhi, "Detection of spam and threads identification in E-mail spam corpus using content based text analytics method," Materials Today: Proceedings, vol. 33, Part 7, pp. 3319-3323, 2020.

[80] Sanjeev Rao, Anil Kumar Verma, and Tarunpreet Bhatia, "Hybrid ensemble framework with self-attention mechanism for social spam detection on imbalanced data," Expert Systems with Applications, vol. 217, pp. 119594, 1 May 2023.

[81] Jenifer Darling Rosita P, and W. Stalin Jacob, "Multi-Objective Genetic Algorithm and CNN-Based Deep Learning Architectural Scheme for effective spam detection," International Journal of Intelligent Networks, vol. 3, pp. 9-15, 2022.

[82] Wessam M. Salama, Moustafa H. Aly, and Yasmine Abouelseoud, "Deep learning-based spam image filtering," Alexandria Engineering Journal, vol. 68, pp. 461-468, 1 April 2023.

[83] Zeynab Fallah Sokhangoee, and Abdoreza Rezapour, "A novel approach for spam detection based on association rule mining and genetic algorithm," Computers & Electrical Engineering, vol. 97, pp. 107655, January 2022.

[84] Giuseppina Andresini, Andrea Iovine, Roberto Gasbarro, Marco Lomolino, Marco de Gemmis, and Annalisa Appice, "EUPHORIA: A neural multi-view approach to combine content and behavioral features in review spam detection," Journal of Computational Mathematics and Data Science, vol. 3, pp. 100036, June 2022.

[85] Bilge Kagan Dedeturk, and Bahriye Akay, "Spam filtering using a logistic regression model trained by an artificial bee colony algorithm," Applied Soft Computing, vol. 91, pp. 106229, June 2020.

[86] S. Jancy Sickory Daisy, and A. Rijuvana Begum, "Smart material to build mail spam filtering technique using Naive Bayes and MRF methodologies," Materials Today: Proceedings, vol. 47, Part 1, pp. 446-452, 2021.

[87] Aakanksha Sharaff, Chandramani Kamal, Siddhartha Porwal, Surbhi Bhatia, Kuljeet Kaur, and Mohammad Mehendi Hassan, "Spam message detection using Danger theory and Krill herd optimization," Computer Networks, vol. 199, pp. 108453, 9 November 2021.

[88] Trivikram Muralidharan, and Nir Nissim, "Improving malicious email detection through novel designated deep-learning architectures utilizing entire email," Neural Networks, vol. 157, pp. 257-279, January 2023.

[89] Sarwat Nizamani, Nasrullah Memon, Mathies Glasdam, and Dong Duong Nguyen, "Detection of fraudulent emails by employing advanced feature abundance," Egyptian Informatics Journal, vol. 15, no. 3, pp. 169-174, November 2014.

[90] Aviad Cohen, Nir Nissim, and Yuval Elovici, "Novel set of general descriptive features for enhanced detection of malicious emails using machine learning methods," Expert Systems with Applications, vol. 110, pp. 143-169, 15 November 2018.

[91] Eman M. Bahgat, Sherine Rady, Walaa Gad, and Ibrahim F. Moawad, "Efficient email classification approach based on semantic methods," Ain Shams Engineering Journal, vol. 9, no. 4, pp. 3259-3269, December 2018.

[92] V. Zorkadis, D.A. Karras, and M. Panayotou, "Efficient information theoretic strategies for classifier combination, feature extraction and performance evaluation in improving false positives and false negatives for spam e-mail filtering," Neural Networks, vol. 18, no. 5–6, pp. 799-807, July–August 2005.

[93] Juan Carlos Gomez, and Marie-Francine Moens, "PCA document reconstruction for email classification," Computational Statistics & Data Analysis, vol. 56, no. 3, pp. 741-751, 1 March 2012.

[94] Ulligaddala Srinivasarao, and Aakanksha Sharaff, "Email thread sentiment sequence identification using PLSA clustering algorithm," Expert Systems with Applications, vol. 193, pp. 116475, 1 May 2022.

[95] Kadam Vikas Samarthrao and Vandana M. Rohokale, "A hybrid metaheuristic- based multi-objective feature selection with adaptive capsule network for automated email spam detection," International Journal of Intelligent Robotics and Applications, vol. 6, pp. 497–521, 2022.

[96] Sunday Olusanya Olatunji, "Improved email spam detection model based on support vector machines," Neural Computing and Applications, vol. 31, pp. 691– 699, 2019.

[97] Ramdane Chikh and Salim Chikhi, "Clustered negative selection algorithm and fruit fly optimization for email spam detection," Journal of Ambient Intelligence and Humanized Computing, vol. 10, pp. 143–152, 2019.

[98] Dataset 1 was available at (https://www.kaggle.com/mandygu/lingspam-dataset)

[99] Dataset 2 was available at (https://www.kaggle.com/venky73/spam-mails-dataset).

[100] Dataset 3 was available at (https://www.kaggle.com/balakishan77/spam-or-ham-email-classification).

[101] Dataset 4 was available at (http://www.cs.jhu.edu/~mdredze/datasets/image_spam/).

[102] Mohammad Jafari and Mohammad Hossein Bayati Chaleshtari, " Using dragonfly algorithm for optimization of orthotropic infinite plates with

a quasi- triangular cut-out", European Journal of Mechanics A/Solids, vol. 66, pp.1-14, 2017.

[103] Fan Li and Manhua Liu, "A hybrid Convolutional and Recurrent Neural Network for Hippocampus Analysis in Alzheimer's Disease", Journal of Neuroscience Methods, vol. 323, pp. 108-118, May 2019.

[104] Dongshu Wang, Dapei Tan, and Lei Liu, "Particle swarm optimization algorithm: an overview," soft computing, vol.22, pp.387-408, 2018.

[105] Seyedali Mirjalili, Seyed Mohammad Mirjalili and Andrew Lewis, "Grey Wolf Optimizer", Advances in Engineering Software, vol.69, pp.46–61, 2014.

[106] SeyedaliMirjalili, and AndrewLewis, "The Whale Optimization Algorithm", Advances in Engineering Software, vol.95, pp.51-67, May 2016.

[107] Bendong Zhao, Huanzhang Lu, Shangfeng Chen, Junliang Liu, and Dongya Wu, "Convolutional neural networks for time series classification", Journal of Systems Engineering and Electronics, vol. 28, no. 1, pp. 162-169, December 2015.

[108] Smith Tsang, Ben Kao, Kevin Y. Yip, Wai-Shing Ho, and Sau Dan Lee, "Decision Trees for Uncertain Data", IEEE Transactions on knowledge and data engineering, vol. 23, no. 1, January 2011.

[109] G. M. Borkar, L. H. Patil, D. Dalgade and A. Hutke,"A novel clustering approach and adaptive SVM classifier for intrusion detection in WSN: A data mining concept,"Sustainable Computing: Informatics and Systems, vol. 23, pp. 120-135, September 2019.

[110] Mingming Huang, Runsheng Lin, Shuai Huang, and Tengfei Xing, "A novel approach for precipitation forecast via improved K-nearest neighbor algorithm,"Advanced Engineering Informatics, vol.33, pp.89-95, August 2017.

[111] Gael Beck, Tarn Duong, Mustapha Lebbah, Hanane Azzag, and Christophe Cerin, "A distributed approximate nearest neighbors algorithm for efficient large scale mean shift clustering,"Journal of Parallel and Distributed Computing, vol.134, pp.128-139, December 2019.

[112] M. Angulakshmi, G.G. Lakshmi Priya, "Walsh Hadamard Transform for Simple Linear Iterative Clustering (SLIC) Superpixel Based Spectral Clustering of Multimodal MRI Brain Tumor Segmentation," IRBM, vol. 40, pp. 253–262, 2019.

[113] Chunhui Zhao, and Furong Gao, "A nested-loop Fisher discriminant analysis algorithm," Chemometrics and Intelligent Laboratory Systems, vol. 146, pp. 396– 406, 2015.

[114] D. Soni and K. J. Mathai, "An Efficient Content Based Image Retrieval System Based on Color Space Approach Using Color Histogram and Color Correlogram," 2015 Fifth International Conference on Communication Systems and Network Technologies, Gwalior, India, 2015.

[115] F. Vernotte, M. Lenczner, P. -Y. Bourgeois and E. Rubiola, "The Parabolic Variance (PVAR): A Wavelet Variance Based on the Least-Square Fit," IEEE Transactions on Ultrasonics, Ferroelectrics, and Frequency Control, vol. 63, no. 4, pp. 611-623, April 2016.

[116] Yanxia Yang, "Research and realization of internet public opinion analysis based on improved TF-IDF algorithm", 16th International Symposium on Distributed Computing and Applications to Business, Engineering and Science, 2017.

[117] X. Cheng, J. He, J. He and H. Xu, "Cv-CapsNet: Complex-Valued Capsule Network," IEEE Access, vol. 7, pp. 85492-85499, 2019.

[118] S.Shadravan, H.R.Naji, and V.K.Bardsiri, "The Sailfish Optimizer: A novel nature-inspired metaheuristic algorithm for solving constrained engineering optimization problems", Engineering Applications of Artificial Intelligence, Vol.80, pp.20-34, April 2019.

[119] Seyedali Mirjalili, Seyed Mohammad Mirjalili and Andrew Lewis, " Grey Wolf Optimizer", Advances in Engineering Software, vol.69, pp.46–61, 2014.

[120] N. P. Nirmala Sreedharan, B. Ganesan, R. Raveendran, P. Sarala, B. Dennis and R. Boothalingam R., "Grey Wolf optimisation-based feature selection and classification for facial emotion recognition," IET Biometrics, vol. 7, no. 5, pp. 490- 499, 9 2018.

[121] Seyedali Mirjalili and Andrew Lewis, " The Whale Optimization Algorithm", Advances in Engineering Software, vol. 95, pp.51–67, 2016.

[122] M. R. Bonyadi and Z. Michalewicz, "Analysis of Stability, Local Convergence, and Transformation Sensitivity of a Variant of the Particle Swarm Optimization Algorithm," IEEE Transactions on Evolutionary Computation, vol. 20, no. 3, pp. 370-385, June 2016.

[123] S. Zhang, X. Li, M. Zong, X. Zhu and R. Wang, "Efficient knn Classification With Different Numbers of Nearest Neighbors," IEEE Transactions on Neural Networks and Learning Systems, vol. 29, no. 5, pp. 1774-1785, May 2018.

[124] S. Tsang, B. Kao, K. Y. Yip, W. Ho and S. D. Lee, "Decision Trees for Uncertain Data," IEEE Transactions on Knowledge and Data Engineering, vol. 23, no. 1, pp. 64-78, Jan. 2011.

[125] J. Wu and H. Yang, "Linear Regression-Based Efficient SVM Learning for Large-Scale Classification," IEEE Transactions on Neural Networks and Learning Systems, vol. 26, no. 10, pp. 2357-2369, Oct. 2015.

[126] D. Wu et al., "Deep Dynamic Neural Networks for Multimodal Gesture Segmentation and Recognition," IEEE Transactions on Pattern Analysis and Machine Intelligence, vol. 38, no. 8, pp. 1583-1597, 1 Aug. 2016.

[127] Q. Song, Y. Wu and Y. C. Soh, "Robust Adaptive Gradient-Descent Training Algorithm for Recurrent Neural Networks in Discrete Time Domain," IEEE Transactions on Neural Networks, vol. 19, no. 11, pp. 1841-1853, Nov. 2008.

[128] K.R. Kruthika, Rajeswari, H.D. Maheshappa, "CBIR System Using Capsule Networks and 3D CNN for Alzheimer's disease Diagnosis," Informatics in Medicine Unlocked, Vol. 14, pp. 59-68, 2019.

[129] H. Zhang, A. Jolfaei and M. Alazab, "A Face Emotion Recognition Method Using Convolutional Neural Network and Image Edge Computing," IEEE Access, vol. 7, pp. 159081-159089, 2019.

[130] Tretyakov K (n.d.) "Machine Learning Techniques in Spam Filtering", Available: https://courses.cs.ut.ee/2004/dm-seminar-spring/uploads/Main/P06.pdf

[131] ShafighAski A, Sourati NK (2016) Proposed efficient algorithm to filter spam using machine learning techniques. Pac Sci Rev A Nat Sci Eng 18(2):145–149.

[132] Mendez JR, Cotos-Yanez TR, Ruano-Ordas D (2019) A new semantic-based feature selection method for spam filtering. Appl Soft Comput J 76:89–104

[133] Subasi A, Alzahrani S, Aljuhani A, Aljedani M (2018) "Comparison of Decision Tree Algorithms for Spam E-mail Filtering," 2018 1st international conference on computer applications & information security (ICCAIS), Riyadh, pp. 1–5

[134] Gupta P, Dubey RK, Mishra S (2019) "Detecting Spam Emails/Sms Using Naive Bayes and Support Vector Machine", Int J Sci Technol Res, Volume 8, Issue 11.

[135] Hassan MA, Mtetwa N (2018) "Feature Extraction and Classification of Spam Emails," 2018 5th international conference on Soft Computing & Machine Intelligence (ISCMI), Nairobi, Kenya, pp. 93–98.

[136] Vanhoenshoven F, Nápoles G, Falcon R, Vanhoof K, K'oppen M (2016) "Detecting malicious URLs using machine learning techniques," 2016 IEEE Symposium Series on Computational Intelligence (SSCI), Athens, pp. 1–8, https://doi.org/10.1109/SSCI.2016.7850079.

[137] Abdulhamid S M, Shuaib M, OluwafemiOsho II, Alhassan JK (2018) Comparative Analysis of Classification Algorithms for Email Spam Detection. Int J Comput Netw Inf Secur (IJCNIS) 10(1):60– 67. https://doi.org/10.5815/ijcnis.2018.01.07

[138] Panigrahi PK (2012) "A Comparative Study of Supervised Machine Learning Techniques for Spam E-mail Filtering," 2012 Fourth International Conference on Computational Intelligence and Communication Networks, pp. 506–512, https://doi.org/10.1109/CICN.2012.14.

[139] Alzahrani A, Rawat DB (2019) "Comparative Study of Machine Learning Algorithms for SMS Spam Detection," 2019 Southeast Con, pp. 1–6, https://doi.org/10.1109/SoutheastCon42311.2019.9020530.

[140] Kontsewaya Y, Antonov E, Artamonov A (2021) Evaluating the effectiveness of machine learning methods for spam detection. Proceeding of Computer Sci 190:479– 486, ISSN 1877-0509. https://doi.org/10.1016/j.procs.2021.06.056

[141] Bassiouni M, Ali M, El-Dahshan EA (2018) Ham and spam E-mails classification using machine learning techniques. J Appl Secur Res 13(3):315–331. https://doi.org/10.1080/19361610.2018.1463136

Index